Muriel Gerhard

The Behavioral Outcomes Handbook:

A Practical Guide
for Teachers and Administrators

Parker Publishing Company, Inc.　　　West Nyack, N.Y.

Library of Congress Cataloging in Publication Data

Gerhard, Muriel.
    The behavioral outcomes handbook.

    Bibliography: p.
    Includes index.
    1. Learning, Psychology of. 2. Behavior
modification. 3. Curriculum planning. I. Title.
LB1051.G437   371.1'02   76-55710
ISBN 0-13-074542-1

Printed in the United States of America

DEDICATION

To: Mark and Michelle
and
all young people
who
value individuality,
appreciate diversity
and
prize humanness

also by the Author:

Effective Teaching Strategies with the Behavioral Outcomes Approach — 1971

A Word from the Author
on the Unique and Practical Value
of This Book

This handbook of practical, down-to-earth effective strategies, activities and classroom-tested resources will enable teachers and administrators to renew and revitalize the process of education, to restore a realistic sense of relevancy to the schools and finally, to bridge the critical gap between the school's current functions and society's ever-increasing demands.

It is written from an experiential base, from working with teachers and administrators who have made firm commitments to promote constructive change, and from interacting with diverse groups of pupils in day-to-day learning situations in actual classrooms under far from ideal conditions. We will deal with the stark realities of change as opposed to the idealistic, utopian pie-in-the-sky educational fantasies which will never be realized in tomorrow's schools, let alone today's schools.

One of the unique things about this book is that it calls for a new, realistic blueprint for education centering on a new curriculum—*an affective-cognitive curriculum which effects changes in the total child.* Education is viewed as a thinking-valuing-individualizing process—a process which focuses not only on the intellectual half of the pupil, but on the affective or emotional half as well. The thrust is on individualized education, integrated in terms of systematically combining affect and cognition, and thereby equipping pupils with not only significant knowledge and fundamental tool skills, but with the intrinsic knowledge of the self—of one's person, feelings, beliefs, attitudes, values and behavioral patterns.

As educators, up to this time we have placed all of our efforts on the education of half of the child—the intellect. We have sometimes

"I Q'd" our schools to almost total irrelevancy. If indeed the latest scores on standardized achievement tests are valid, we have demonstrated our failure. We have ignored half of the pupil, a crucial half, the half that activates, motivates, seeks satisfaction, internalizes success or failure, and identifies with being, becoming, growing and self-actualization.

For decades we have espoused the concept of the whole child. We have read about the concept, conferenced about the concept, discussed it and verbally accepted it. It is time we moved from the discussion level to the action level. The hard empirical data are here: the drug crisis, the literacy crisis, the identity crisis, the growing disenchantment with education. Need we go on? Our energies have been well dissipated in this continuous crisis-hopping cycle. A new blueprint for education is needed, one which provides for the education of the total child. Can this be done? Do we have the skills and the resources to accomplish this goal? The answer is, emphatically, yes! How this is done is the substance of this book.

The approach which is utilized is a modification of the Behavioral Outcomes Approach, which was first utilized to promote the use of process skills in the cognitive domain. Its initial success and its unanticipated effects in terms of affective outcomes led to its direct application to the affective domain. The early critics of the Behavioral Outcomes Approach clearly stated that it *had not gone far enough. The process skills were certainly equally applicable to the affective domain.* Before long, school systems who had followed the Norwalk original Behavioral Outcomes Plan made modifications and found that the changes were not only dramatically positive, but that processing both cognitive and affective data reinforced the totality of the learning structures. Cognitive and affective structures were interwoven and an affective-cognitive curriculum was the most effective vehicle for the development of the whole child.

This Behavioral Outcomes Handbook provides teachers and administrators with the detailed step-by-step procedures and with clear-cut operational definitions to achieve this goal.

Specifically, as a result of utilizing this handbook, you will be able to:

- Implement the modified Behavioral Outcomes Approach which focuses on the use of process skills and applies these skills to both the cognitive and affective domains of learning.
- Promote relevant affective learning by developing positive self-concepts in pupils and fostering an awareness and clarification of feelings, beliefs, attitudes and values.

- Understand and capitalize on the new generation's search for a "role" identity and thereby be able to reshape the instructional process for an "Identity Society."
- Apply effective classroom strategies activities and questioning techniques to promote more objective thinking and greater values clarification, resulting in an increased understanding of the "what's," "why's," and "how's" of these processes.
- Construct practical and significant behavioral objectives in the affective domain.
- Modify your existing curriculum and create an integrated and balanced affective and cognitive curriculum.
- Develop specific affective and cognitive teaching competencies in order to implement this curriculum.
- Implement a practical instructional system that individualizes, cognitively and affectively, allowing for the development and growth of the whole person.

In sum, this handbook provides you with the essential tools, strategies and resources to implement this new blueprint which will have a significant impact on the education of our young. The changes outlined in the book—by no means drastic or radical—are long over-due. They are realistic and attainable. They reflect the needs of our times. As professionals, we cannot close our eyes to these needs. We cannot turn our backs on our young people, for we do have a mission far greater than any yet achieved—that of reaching our young, of educating them to the fullest extent. Perhaps I have an excess of faith in teachers, and in educators—but I doubt it!

Muriel Gerhard

ACKNOWLEDGMENTS

I owe the formulation of this book to the numerous teachers and administrators in Connecticut who were active participants in the initial Behavioral Outcomes Program, in Project AMP and in the Modified Behavioral Outcomes Program. Their receptivity to new ideas and their willingness to give of their time and energy were the major factors contributing to the program's success. I am especially indebted to the numerous school systems in New Jersey and New York who were inspired to implement the Behavioral Outcomes Program and welcomed the opportunity to expand it into the affective domain. Their affective perceptions and efforts were indeed effective.

My fullest measure of gratitude is to my husband and my children, whose interest, encouragement, support and understanding made this an exciting endeavor.

CONTENTS

"Getting down to basics". . . .Our changing
society. . . .Avoiding the "Where-did-we-go-
wrong?" syndrome . . . . Examining the past and
present of educational change. . . .The basis for a
new blueprint. . . .The message. . . .Developing affective and cognitive curriculum. . . .Curricular
adaptation and the development of teacher competencies. . . .Focusing on the in-
dividual. . . .Providing for individualization of the
whole child. . . .Developing a strong, positive self-
image. . . .The need for self-identity. . . .The
school's role. . . .The new blueprint for education.

Self-concept: The affective key to learning. . . .Developing a sense of worth. . . .Learning
to cope. . . .Expressing feelings and
emotions. . . .How the expression of feelings and
emotions affect self-concept. . . .Developing a
sense of autonomy. . . .The new generation's
search for role. . . .Creating a responsive learning
environment. . . .The self-fulfilling prophecy in
operation. . . .How to use the behavioral outcomes
approach to promote a positive self-concept.

Chapter 5 — Completing the Affective Cycle . . . . . .

Structuring questions for general interpretation. . . .Structuring questions for affective interpretation. . . .Strategies for affective interpretation. . . .Expressing personal meaning. . . .Constructing inferences. . . .Making predictions. . . .Applying interpretation strategies to curricular content. . . .Sample applications for elementary, intermediate and secondary pupils. . . .Generalizing. . . .Dealing with issues. . . .Applying divergent strategies to curricular content. . . .Critical thinking. . . .Creative strategies for developing self-concept. . . .Creative strategies for exploration of feelings beliefs and values. . . .Apply these strategies to personal and curricular content. . . .Concept formation. . . .Defining a concept. . . .Conceptualizing. . . .Strategies for concept formation in the affective and cognitive domain. . . .Expanding pupils' concepts. . . .Sample applications of concept formation.

Chapter 6 — How to Begin Specifying Objectives in the Affective Domain . . . .

Updating our progress. . . .Integrating affective goals and objectives into the curriculum. . . .Objectives—"New and improved". . . .Reassessing the practical worth of goals and objectives. . . .The status of objectives. . . .Obtaining a working knowledge of affective objectives. . . .General guidelines in writing objectives. . . .Utilizing working papers. . . .Affective goals vs. affective objectives. . . .Designating behaviors. . . .Differentiating between overt and covert behaviors. . . ."Unmixing the Behavioral Mix". . . .Operational terminology for affective description.

Chapter 7 — Completing the Construction of Affective Objectives . . . .

Performance objectives. . . .Performance objectives in the affective domain. . . .Direct and in-

devices. . . .The essential pupil skills for
individualization—self-instruction and self-
evaluation. . . .The seven major areas of self-
direction. . . .Specific self-directive pupil
behaviors. . . .Applying the "III" Model to a classroom situation.

The "Schools for Children" concept. . . .Key questions and procedures for teachers. . . .Creating the
most responsive environment. . . .Pre-testing,
analysis and modification. . . .Implementing the
Learning Unit. . . .Sharing the results. . . .Practical
guidelines for administrators. . . .Shared
leadership and shared responsibility. . . .Involving
teachers in the decision-making pro-
cess. . . .Conclusion.

1 A New Blueprint for Education

"Getting Down to Basics"

Educators are busy people, and busy people get down to basics. In fact, the term "getting down to basics" appears to have gained popularity in our society today. There are those who attempt to convince us that the major facets of our lives will improve if we get down to basics. The message is direct and full of impact. The tragedy lies in the superficiality of some "basics" and the falseness of many claims.

For educators, this message is not new. We have been attempting for decades to get down to basics in order to provide the best education for all, yet despite our extensive efforts, the solution has eluded us. What should be basic to the education of all? What combination of knowledge, skills, attitudes and values will insure a large measure of success in life? It is obvious that we have not hit upon the right combination. The critics have told us that our basics are superficial and lack relevancy, and that our mix is flagrantly inadequate. In sum, our product is not meeting the critical needs of society as it exists today.

Our Changing Society

Outwardly and inwardly, the face and the essence of our society have changed drastically. The rate and scope of change have been unprecedented. We have no need to research this; the hard data is bombarding us from all directions. This world of ours is not what it used to be! Knowledge, technology, ethics, morals, values, lifestyles have changed, are changing, and in all probability will continue to change. We continuously ask ourselves: have we changed—as educators, as parents, as human beings? Have we changed to the extent that we are able to cope realistically and successfully with the ever-emerging new conditions, problems and crises? Have we been looking at education and society through outdated cognitive systems and obsolete value systems? Are our perceptions congruent with the realities?

The "Where-Did-We-Go-Wrong?" Syndrome

We have valid reasons to question. Listening to our colleagues, to parents and neighbors, we hear the same question again and again and again ad nauseam, "Where did we go wrong?" This "Where-did-we-go-wrong" syndrome is being applied to our political, economic, health and welfare systems, but its main thrust is upon our educational system.

There is no doubt that education has not kept in step with the times and that as it is practiced today, it does not mirror our society, but this is a general response to "Where did we go wrong?" As practitioners we have found that generalities are of little practical value unless they are translated into specific operations. To get down to specifics we need to reexamine the process of education: its past, present and future. We therefore confront those old familiar questions: Where have we been? Where are we now? Where are we going?

Examining the Past and Present of Educational Change

We have been in the past where the rate and scope of change have not been drastic, where the old philosophies, goals, organizational patterns, methodologies and curricular resources appeared to yield positive results, and where the inadequacies of education were not flagrant.

Where are we now? We are at various points along a continuum of change, for receptivity to change has increased significantly in the last decade. Although there are the few who are still guarding the past, reluctant to change, rationalizing, fearful of implementing "faddish" innovations, the majority are involved in the change process. Of this majority, a small segment is involved in testing innovations, adapting and tailoring them to their perceived needs, searching for sound empirical evidence with which to evaluate their actions to direct or redirect their future plans. Unfortunately, a large segment is floundering in a patchwork of innovations, unable to validly assess their results, searching for direction and asking, "Are we really going anywhere?" Obviously, despite the increase in innovative attitudes and practices the glaring inadequacies of our present system persist.

Basis for a New Blueprint

Logically, these key questions arise: Where are we going? Where can we go? What is our blueprint for the future? Upon what basic assumptions do we formulate it? Where do we start?

We start in the here and now. We start by developing a new perspective of what the school's functions must be in the context of this society and its young: society as it exists beset with its critical problems, and its young people as they are, feel, perceive, think, value or do not value, function or do not function, cope or do not cope. A large percentage of our young are alienated, frustrated and searching for their own value systems, identities and goals, tossing aside the goals, ethical codes and value systems we embraced so unquestionably.

Our young show great concern about the human condition. Via the media, they have seen poverty, war, death, racial riots, ecological and political corruption. They see little or no value in material acquisitions and in career status. They have begun to question the value and relevance of formal education to prepare them for coping with the critical social problems arising from a complex technological society. They have rejected our schools. Their attitudes have become increasingly negative toward the school, teachers and "academe." Whatever feelings we harbor matter little at this point. To use a current cliche, this is where it's at! What matters is the message we are receiving and its direct implications for a new blueprint for education.

The Message Is Clear

The message we are receiving is evident, namely that *education, if it is to achieve relevancy, must be time bound and must be contextual in character.* In brief, it must match the times and needs. The times are characterized by new problems requiring new solutions, by changing value systems demanding a reassessment of old values and the recreation of value systems relevant to the present.

Developing Affective and Cognitive Behaviors

The first component of our new blueprint is equally evident. *Schools must concern themselves with affective behaviors. Feelings, emotions, attitudes, values, beliefs, interests and appreciations are major concerns of current education.*

If we re-examine the past and the present of education, we find that for decades we have been educating *one quarter of the child* by providing the so-called "basic skills" and knowledges. We taught or attempted to teach the three Rs and to impart knowledge in the major disciplines. In the last decade we have become keenly aware of cognitive learning. The movement as in the original Behavioral Outcomes Approach[1], has been away from low-level cognition, rote learning and memorization, and toward higher cognitive processes. We have discovered that children can think, do think and are capable of demonstrating significant growth in the thinking processes. The focus has been on learning to learn, processing knowledge, internalizing knowledge, developing conceptual frameworks and expanding these frameworks. The concept of the child as a passive receptacle for tool skills and knowledge has been replaced by the child as an active processer of knowledge and skills. He is a thinking individual capable of applying these processes not only to his formal education, but to life situations. In the cognitive domain, he is becoming his own man.

From my past experiences as director of the Behavioral Outcomes Program which focused on cognitive learning, I believe that we have come a long way in education. The results of our study indicated that teachers, administrators, parents and, most importantly, pupils, were extremely responsive to process learning. Schools were becoming stimulating environments conducive to cognitive growth. Teachers were constructing cognitive curricula, using cognitive teaching strategies, asking thought-provoking questions. Attitudes towards school and learning were becoming increasingly positive. The cognitive focus was producing affective results. We knew at an intellectual level that cognition was but one half of the human domain and that affect was the other, and what was occuring in the classroom was the continuous interaction of the two. They were not separate and distinct entities, but were integrated. They operated together, one reinforcing the other. We are not rational or emotive individuals; we are rational-emotive beings. We think and we feel. Our thoughts influence our emotions and conversely our emotions influence our thoughts and the interaction of both determine our behavior. Rarely, if ever, do we operate totally in the cognitive or affective domain. The focus on cognition is definitely a step in the right

1. Muriel Gerhard *Effective Teaching Strategies with the Behavioral Outcomes Approach.* West Nyack, N.Y.: Parker Publishing Company, Inc., 1971.

direction, but it is not enough! A cognitive focus results in the education of one-half of the child, the intellectual half. What our young people have been saying in very explicit terms is that affect is as vital as cognition, that society's problems have both affective and cognitive components and that we live our lives at both the intellectual and gut levels. For countless years we have been talking about the education of the whole child. Now we know what is required of us: the development of both halves, the promotion of cognitive *and* affective behaviors.

Creating a Balanced Affective and Cognitive Curriculum

To reiterate, the first component of our blueprint is: *We must promote the development of affective behaviors.* The second component of our blueprint deals with the other half of the child: *We must continue to foster the growth of cognitive behaviors.* If cognitive and affective development are our goals, the third component of our blueprint must deal with the means. Yes, we know what it says, but how is it done? *We must modify our curriculum so that the resultant product is a balanced affective and cognitive curriculum.*

This task is not a new one, nor is it insurmountable. Extensive work has been done in both domains. Operational cognitive curricula and cognitive teaching strategies have been developed and successfully implemented in the Behavioral Outcomes Program. In the affective domain, the work of the late Hilda Taba, of Louis Raths, Sidney Simon, Merrill Harmon, Howard Kirschenbaum, Leland Howe, William Glasser, Richard Jones, J.J. Gordon and Robert Samples has yielded excellent materials, procedures, strategies for realistic classroom implementation.

The affective and cognitive domains are dealt with extensively in this handbook. Models of affective and cognitive curricula and more importantly integrated affective and cognitive curricula are provided. Specific procedures, teaching strategies, questioning sequences, pupil activities are described in detail. Numerous samples in the various disciplines are included.

Curricular Adaptation and the
Development of Teacher Competencies

The task in utilizing these models and practices is twofold: one, of adapting this integrated curriculum to your specific school environment and modifying it to meet the needs of pupils and teachers; and two, of developing competency in the use of the strategies and techniques so that the process of implementation is natural rather than artificial and contrived.

Curricular adaptation and modification are processes experienced teachers have always practiced. There is no one curriculum which will meet all of the needs of our diverse pupil population. Reality dictates continuous adaptation and modification.

As for the need for the development of teacher competencies, past experience has clearly demonstrated that we may have the finest curricular vehicle to achieve the most relevant goals and objectives, but unless we have the know-how, unless we have the skills to operate that vehicle, we will be unable to reach our destination. Therefore the fourth component of our blueprint is crucial to implementation: *We must develop specific affective and cognitive teaching competencies in order to implement this curriculum.*

In this handbook you will not find mere descriptions of these competencies. To read about them is one thing; to be able to use them effectively is another. What you will find will be operational definitions of these competencies, telling you specifically, in concrete terms, what you are going to do, and why and how you are going to do it. In sum, you will be given the operations you are to perform, the rationale for these operations and a variety of contexts in which to perform. You will develop these skills by experiencing them. Is there a better way?

As a consultant to numerous school systems, I have found that most teachers tend to teach in the manner in which they were taught. Only when they are provided with hands-on experiences and take on the role of the pupil do they develop the kinds of insights and understanding which dramatically change their teaching behaviors. There seems to be no substitute for the experiential method in promoting behavioral change.

Focusing on the Individual

The fifth component of our blueprint is inherent in our goals. If our goals are to develop young people who have the skills enabling them to think for themselves, to keep in touch with their feelings and attitudinal sets, clarify their values and reconstruct value systems in keeping with the times, then our focus is on the individual.

Although in educational practice we instruct a class, a class does not think—an individual does. A class does not feel or value—an individual does. In act, in the learning context the class does little, if anything except persist as a myth. We have been so brainwashed over the years that this illusion of the class as a learning entity has become a reality.

As experienced teachers, we know all too well that a class does not learn; it is the individual in the class who learns or does not learn. Our problem has been in the instructional context—namely with the increasing number of individuals we are given to work with simultaneously. This group of individuals unfortunately has been given the label of class, carrying with it fallacious and detrimental implications, but the reality exists and persists. We are dealing with individuals who possess differences in learning styles, learning rates, learning modalities, drives, motivation, and feelings about themselves and about the world in general. All of these differences have a profound effect on both the learning and teaching processes. If learning is a unique and individualized process, then the teaching or instructional process must follow suit. Therefore, *we must provide an instructional system that is truly individualizing, geared to these differences in both the cognitive and affective domains.*

The term *individualized instruction* has become a platitude, a cliche which has been overused and abused. The concept of individualization has been subjected to so many diverse interpretations that for the majority of educational practitioners it has been reduced to a meaningless pie-in-the-sky, utopian ideal.

Attempts at implementation have varied from: the use of programmed instruction where children live in a world of paper and pencil diagnosis, paper and pencil instruction, paper and pencil evaluation—the use of LAPS, learning activity packets, where the paper and pencil structures still persist but are augmented with some activities to computer-assisted instruction where costs are so prohibitive that few may benefit. For the most part, individualized instruction has been directed at skill learning, rote learning and low-level concept formation. The major efforts have been in the development of basic, broad tool skills such as the three Rs.

Providing for Individualization of the Whole Child

Individualization has been directed or, I should say, misdirected at barely half of the child. If we are sincere in our efforts—and we are—what is needed is not partial individualization, but complete and real individualization which focuses not only on "cognitive" development but on affective development as well. In education it is so easy to become bogged down with mechanistic details that we can readily lose sight of our goal of educating the complete individual, the whole person. The fifth component of our blueprint—that of *providing for the individualization of the whole child*—is a major one.

It would take little effort to teach for both domains by using the typical rote, didactic, direct, authoritarian-centered, shotgun methods of the past, directed at the class, the group, the mass. The results would be no better than what has been achieved; in fact they would be far worse. We would be substituting indoctrination for individualization in two domains. The name of the game would be Know What I Know, Think As I Think, Value As I Value, Become What I Am! History has clearly shown us the results of indoctrination. As American educators, we have taken pride in the fact that our schools' major function is to educate rather than indoctrinate or train. For us, education has meant providing opportunities for the whole development of every individual based on his or her potential. What is required, then, is the fifth component of our blueprint: *We must provide an instructional system that individualizes cognitively and affectively, allowing for the development and growth of the whole person.*

In this handbook, the process of individualized instruction as it applies to the cognitive and affective domains is dealt with at a practical level for direct application in the classroom. The key components of individualization are spelled out as concrete operations. You are given a description of an individualizing classroom so that you can readily understand how it differs from a conventional one. You are provided with an operational listing of individualizing teaching skills so that you have a clear-cut picture of how the individualizing teacher performs. The pupil skills required for individualization are delineated so that you can adequately prepare your pupils for successful entry into the program. The how-to procedures, such as how teachers convert regular curricular material and resources into individualizing ones, how the Behavioral Outcomes Approach is used, how assessments are made of individualizing practices and pupil outcomes, and how administrators and supervisors provide supportive services, are all presented in tangible, substantive and down-to-earth terms. In sum, individualized instruction, as it is described in this handbook, has been tailored to fit actual teachers operating in normal classrooms under realistic conditions. This is no educational version of "Mission Impossible." The means are functional and the results are attainable!

Developing a Strong, Positive Self-Image

The sixth component of our blueprint is the key component: *We must provide maximum opportunities to enable the individual to develop a strong, positive self-image.* This component is closely related to our first component: the development of affective behaviors, the concern with the individual's feelings, emotions, attitudes, values, beliefs, interests and appreciations.

Today's popular literature has certainly reinforced the fact that we are our own best friend and that this need to be our own best friend is very real. Whether we turn to philosophical writings or psychological texts, well-known sayings and expressions of principles such as "Know thyself," "If I am not for myself, who will be for me?", "there is a real self to be discovered and actualized" are not mere quotations or meaningless platitudes. They point up the knowledge that is of most worth, the knowledge that is basic to survival, growth, achievement and the process of living in all of its aspects. We may call it inner knowledge; personal knowledge; a knowledge of one's self, one's identity, being or worth.

If we have this sense of identity and of self-worth; if we know who we are, what we are, and what we stand for; if we view ourselves as somebodies, then we are prepared to function as healthy, constructive human beings. If, on the other hand, we lack this sense of identity, view ourselves as nobodies, of little value to ourselves or others, not knowing what we are, confused about what we value—if anything, incapable of being accepted by others, having friends, doing worthwhile things, then we are at a loss to function. If we are unable to find ourselves and value ourselves, how can we find a place in society and be valued by society?

How we see ourselves determines how we see the world around us and how we interact with it. In sum, if we have a strong, positive self-image, if we identify ourselves as unique individuals, capable of success, then we will strive for success. But—if we view ourselves as nonentities, or failures, we will identify with failure and operate as failures.

The Need for Self-Identity

Obviously, this need for self-identity has always existed. But, the fact is—that in this new society characterized by excessive specialization and technology, the need to be recognized as individuals is greater than ever before. This is not only true for the young but for the middle-aged and old as well. This fact is mirrored in the media. "You, you're the one!" and "I don't mind paying more for X shampoo, I'm worth it!" All of us are given the message, whatever our age: "You are important; you are unique; you are a person; you should care about yourself; you matter!"

The School's Role

But where should the seed of "You are a person! You matter!" be planted? The response is obvious: in our schools where the young have their early experiences of success or failure, where they begin to find themselves. We cannot question the value of the sixth component of our blueprint: *to develop a strong, positive self-image in the child.* We need schools which provide children with opportunities to succeed, to be involved with their peers, to develop friends, to do worthwhile things, to reinforce a positive self-image, a sense of accomplishment, a sense of worth, a sense of competency, a sense of being liked and accepted for being themselves.

How this can be accomplished and is being accomplished is described in Chapter 2. You are provided with basic principles, strategies, techniques and procedures for assisting the pupil in developing a positive self-concept. Continuous application of these procedures in the classroom will demonstrate their value. To date, this goal has not received the attention it demands. It is up to us—teachers and administrators—to concentrate our efforts on the goal of role reinforcement. For, as our young people understand their individual roles as persons having their own identities, only then will they be able to determine their goals in society.

The New Blueprint for Education

Our task has been to "get down to basics," to determine a new blueprint for education in the context of this society and its most pressing needs. The blueprint consists of the following six components:

- We must concern ourselves with affective behaviors. Feelings, emotions, attitudes, values, beliefs, interests and appreciations are major concerns of current education.
- We must continue to foster the growth of cognitive behaviors. New problems will demand new solutions requiring the use of cognitive processes.
- We must modify our curriculum so that the resultant product is a balanced affective and cognitive curriculum.
- We must develop specific affective and cognitive teaching competencies in order to implement this curriculum.
- We must provide an instructional system that individualizes, cognitively and affectively, allowing for the development and growth of the whole person.

- We must provide maximum opportunities to enable the individual to develop a strong and positive self-image.

Summary

These in essence are our goals. The rationale for each one has been given. The specific procedures and strategies are provided in this handbook. What occurs is up to us. We are equipped with realistic, relevant goals, and the essential methods of operation. We are cognizant of the fact that knowledge, in and of itself, is of little value unless it is applied—put into realistic practice. We are well aware of the need to close the cultural gap between educational practice and society's needs, and are an extremely capable people. We have made great strides in space and have reached the moon, but we have yet to make those strides in education and reach our children. Yesterday, the moon; tomorrow, our children. The mission is ours!

2 Promoting Affective Learning with the Behavioral Outcomes Approach

Self-Concept: The Affective Key to Learning

In the first chapter we identified the key component of our new blueprint for education as promoting the development of a strong and positive self-image. The rationale for focusing on self-image or self-concept has been presented briefly. The changing needs of our society, the obvious failure of our schools, the increase in crime and violence, drug addiction, alcoholism have compelled us to look more closely at what we as educators have been doing and not doing. Now more than ever before we must deal with the whole child, not only with his cognitive behaviors, cognitive achievements and intellectual maturity, but with his affective behaviors, affective achievements and his emotional maturity.

For years educators and psychologists have spoken of the significance of self-concept in human development. We have only to look at the writings of Carl Rogers, Abraham Maslow, Arthur Combs, Daniel Prescot, Magda Arnold, Rodney Clark, Walcott Beatty—and countless others—to substantiate this fact. In the day-to-day process of education, we have failed to view it as central to learning—as the key to learning. We have dealt with it as an abstraction, while its concrete effects have been dramatically felt and demonstrated.

To deal with something in concrete terms, we must first view it in concrete terms. What is a self-concept? It is a set of images which each of us has about himself or herself. It is how you and I perceive ourselves, wheher we see ourselves as unique individuals who are liked, loved, accepted by others, worthy or unworthy, adequate or inadequate, able to cope with experience, having control of our lives or being manipulated by people or events. All of these self-perceptions, real or unreal, make up our self-concept. Whether they are real or un real is of little significance. If we perceive them as real, they are real for us. What we have done—each of us in our own way—has been to organize our experiences and our learnings, both affective and cognitive, into an image or concept of what we are at the present time. Based on the extensive work of Rodney Clark and Walcott Beatty,[1] our unified self-concept can be viewed as consisting of four major senses or abilities: our sense of worth, our perceived ability to cope, our ability to express our feelings and emotions, and our sense of autonomy.

Developing a Sense of Worth

Let's examine each of these senses and abilities. First, what constitutes a sense of worth? What makes an individual feel worthy? How can we develop this in an individual? We feel a sense of worth when we are liked, accepted by others, loved, are included or belong, and are given priority over other things. We develop a sense of worth when our friends, family and teachers demonstrate this liking, acceptance, caring for and valuing of the individual. These behaviors communicate to the individual the message "you count, you matter, you are a special person—you are worthy of being."

A story which comes to mind and exemplifies teaching behavior which fosters this sense of worth was related at an ASCD convention by Dr. Arthur Combs. Dr. Combs was talking about an affective or humanistic teacher and how this teacher functions in the classroom.

Dr. Combs was visiting an elementary school. As he walked through the halls, escorted by the principal, a young boy came running toward them with tears streaming down his face. "I lost my teacher!" he cried. The principal assured him that they would find his teacher and asked for a description of his teacher. "She has long blonde hair hanging down her back," was the reply. So the three continued down the hall looking into classrooms until lo and behold— the long blonde hair.

The teacher turned and saw the child. She raced across the room, put her arms around the child and said, "Oh Tommy, where were you? We missed you!"

She could have said, "Tommy you are late! Go to the office and

---

1. Walcott H. Beatty and Rodney A. Clark, "A Self Concept Theory of Learning." Monograph, San Francisco State College, 1962. Reprinted in: Henry C. Lindgren. *Readings in Educational Psychology*. New York: John Wiley & Sons, Inc., 1968.

get a late pass!" This would have been the behavior of a procedure-oriented teacher. Or she could have said, "Tommy you have missed doing page 10 in your workbook. Get in here right this minute and get to work!" This would have been the behavior of a task-oriented teacher. Or she could have invited the principal and esteemed guest in, saying, "Won't you come in and see what we are doing?" This is the administratively oriented teacher: teacher today, administrator tomorrow.

But she was the humanistic teacher. Her response was "We missed you!" Her message was: You are an important person to us; we care about you; you are worthy of our concern.

Our sense of worth, then, is nurtured by the behaviors of others and by our perceptions of these behaviors. If we are fortunate in being liked, accepted, included and valued, these experiences enhance our sense of worth. If our experiences are negative, those of rejection and exclusion, we experience feelings of dissatisfaction and even pain—for we want to be worthy. Our dissatisfaction or pain may motivate us to change our behaviors or to find other ways to obtain appreciation, love and acceptance.

The extent of our efforts is determined by the size of the gap between the ideal image of self-worth which we have constructed and which we strive to attain and our perceived image. If most of our experiences have reinforced our sense of worth, the gap between the ideal and the perceived image is small. We feel confident in bridging the gap and our efforts continue. However, if our experiences have been consistently negative over a long period of time, we may perceive ourselves as totally worthless. "I am a bad person; no one likes me! If I were a good person, people would like me! Why bother? I give up!" The gap is viewed as too large to span. The why-bother-I-can't-make-it attitude results. We retreat; we escape. We may even give up the hope of ever regaining our sense of worth.

Learning to Cope

The second major facet of self-concept is our perceived ability to cope. How we cope with daily experiences and the extent to which we cope successfully, based on the various kinds of feedback we receive, determine our perception of our coping ability. None of us can argue the point that in today's society the amount and kinds of coping ability necessary are so great that schools must provide assistance in developing these skills.

In learning to cope, we have models: our peers, family, teachers, friends and leaders. We develop not only a perception of our own coping ability, but we construct an ideal image of coping ability toward which we work. As in the case of our sense of worth, we are reinforced in our responses by the outside world. If the discrepancy or gap between the perceived and the ideal are not too great, we are motivated to increase our efforts. If the discrepancy is too large, overwhelming, unattainable by our standards, we reduce our efforts or abandon them completely.

Too often the sense of worth becomes intertwined with the sense of coping. We have seen parents and educators withhold affection, grades or rewards to "motivate" the child to meet their expectations. What occurs is psychologically damaging, for one's worth now depends on doing what others dictate, not on our goals, decisions and values. We are bribed to attain our worth and it is no longer our true worth. What a drastic price to pay!

Expressing Feelings and Emotions

The third major facet of self-concept is the ability to express our feelings and emotions. It is essential that we differentiate between a feeling and an emotion. A feeling is a mild emotion; its intensity can be plotted along a continuum ranging from unpleasant at one pole to pleasant at the other pole. An emotion is a strong bodily reaction and has a far greater range of intensity. Emotions usually impel us to act. The resultant actions may be mild, strong or totally disorganizing.

Traditionally our society and our schools have suppressed the expression of feelings and emotions. As students we were taught to intellectualize our feelings and emotions. A display of feelings or emotions rarely received approval. "Don't get emotional! Control yourself! You are not being rational about this! We must not show our feelings!" were the characteristic reprimands.

We can generalize that most people do not wish to view or share anger or grief or even extreme happiness. The expression of feelings and emotions carry with them a large element of disturbance. This threat of disturbance is evident when we consider the fact that emotions are strong feelings, may be released suddenly, arousing one to action, and that the resultant actions may be unpredictable. However, when feelings have been suppressed rather than expressed, when they have been bottled up and reach such intensity that they are explosive in nature, we may realistically anticipate that the results may be frightening and threatening.

At a superficial level, it seems far wiser to encourage emotional control, to intellectualize feelings and emotions in the false hope that in submerging them they will be fully dissipated. Unfortunately this is not the case. The emotional energy cannot be stored or condensed; it must be released. We must acknowledge that as fully functioning human beings, we experience feelings that are pleasant or unpleasant, satisfying or unsatisfying; that we find ourselves in situations which evoke strong emotional responses and that this is a natural process.

How the Expression of Feelings and Emotion
Affect Self-Concept

To fully understand the value of feelings and emotions and their crucial role in affecting our behavior, we must view them in terms of their relationship to our self-concept. Let's assume that in our daily life, we come in contact with information and experiences that are irrelevant to our self-concept. This specific information and these happenings have no effect upon our senses of worth, of coping, and of autonomy. They are insignificant. We experience boredom.

However, if our daily encounters are such that they are relevant and congruent with our self-concept—with our senses of worth, coping and autonomy—and reinforce them, we are now more worthy, better able to cope, more autonomous. We then experience pleasant feelings or even emotions of joy.

On the other hand, if these daily encounters are inconsistent and incongruent with our self-concept and our sense of self, causing us to perceive ourselves as less worthy, unable to cope adequately or less autonomous, then we may experience feelings that are unpleasant or emotions which are painful. In essence, how our daily experiences match or mismatch our senses of self, our senses of worth, coping and autonomy, and determine the kind and degree of feelings and emotions generated. These feelings and emotions, once they are expressed, clarified and accepted, dictate our future behavior.

If our feelings are pleasant or joyous we "go to it!"—we move ahead, we increase our efforts. If our feelings are unpleasant, we may stop to reassess what we have been doing, why we have been doing it, and what options are available to us. We may pause and reflect. However, if the impact has been strongly negative, we may experience depression. We may screech to a halt, retreat, attempt to escape or lapse into doing nothing.

We cannot overestimate the role and value of feelings and emotions and their effects on our functioning. They serve as a personal barometer. They are activators and deactivators of behavior, critical guides to personal behavior modification, and indispensable tools.

To be able to use a tool we must be familiar with it. Therefore, unless we are more than familiar—unless we experience, express, accept, clarify and thereby know our feelings, we are not in touch with our real selves. We pride ourselves on being realists. We ask our children to be realistic; how much more realistic can we get than to confront the realities of ourselves?

The implications for education are apparent, but these implications have very definite parameters. Teachers are not psychiatrists or psychologists, nor do we claim to be. Our role is not one of delving or probing the psychic depths of the individual. Psychoanalysis is one thing; developing a healthy and strong self-concept is another. If we view our role as enabling pupils to express their feelings and emotions, to accept them, clarify them and understand them through the vehicles of the literary arts, the social sciences, the physical sciences, arts, music and dance, we are not treading on dangerous ground nor are we opening Pandora's Box; in fact, we might be closing Pandora's Box. In sum, the expression of feelings and emotions within the constructive channels of the school, not their suppression, is the answer.

Developing a Sense of Autonomy

The fourth major facet of self-concept is the sense of autonomy—the feeling that we have control over our lives, that we have options and alternatives, that we are capable of making choices, decisions and determinations about our future.

Simply from the viewpoint of mental health, we would assume that a strong sense of autonomy would enhance our ability to function in a society which values the individual. It is not surprising, therefore, that research clearly indicates that our motivation in any learning environment increases if we feel we have some measure of control over it. Practical experience extends and substantiates this finding. We are motivated to and do work harder in any environment—home or business—where we "have a say," where our inputs are given real consideration and where we have "a piece of the action" and some voice in and control of that action.

What is surprising is that despite the great value that educators have verbally placed on individual autonomy, the schools have done little to foster it, but much to negate it.

As teachers there is little doubt in our minds that the future of the democratic process depends upon individuals who can and do exercise and maintain control over their lives, see options and alternatives and seek data so that they are capable of making informed choices and valid decisions and can assume the responsibilities for these decisions and their consequences. This, in essence, is what our young are told is required of them. This is what is preached; but what is practiced in our schools?

The Effects of Autonomy on Motivation and Discipline

Most of us who made the trip on student fare found that conformity not autnomy was fostered and rewarded. We were given few if any options or alternatives. We had two options—pass or fail—which translated into operational terms were simply: Do as we say and you will pass, and don't do as we say and you will fail.

As for decision making, this was a totally foreign realm to most of us. Decisions were made for us not by us. We carried them out. We took orders, followed directions and were rewarded with letters of the alphabet, two and three digit numerals and gold geometric configurations. Controlled conformity, not autonomous individuality, was practiced. This was viewed as essential if discipline was to be maintained.

What is startling is that children who are provided with opportunities to become autonomous are motivated to learn, and that children who are motivated to learn have little time to become discipline problems. They are involved with learning, not raising the roof. In fact, they develop and demonstrate a self-discipline which is far more effective than the extrinsic variety imposed by the school. We may well question what realistic gains were made by this negation of autonomy and this drastic need for disciplined conformity, but that was the past, or so we hope to believe. Autonomous individuals should be the products of our schools—not the by-products!

Educating for Autonomy

The task of educating for autonomy is by no means an easy one. We would be naive if we viewed it as such. Just as we can't make people free, we can't make people autonomous. We can only provide the environment, guidance, opportunities and resources to enable the person to free himself or gain autonomy.

I am reminded of a cartoon depicting a man with a large ball and chain ensconcing his ankle. The chain has been cut. The man is standing there, inspecting the cut chain with a distraught expression on his face. The caption reads, "What do I do now?" Doesn't this remind you of youngsters you have taught? I can look back and see some of my students with a variety of captions: "Tell me!" "Show me!" "Lead me!" "Hey, I'm stuck!"

How many of our students have been told, shown, led, directed, become so accustomed to our help that the thought of coping by themselves is frightening, anxiety-ridden and frustrating. In promoting autonomous behavior, we realize all too soon that individual differences do exist, that children require various degrees and kinds of structure and support. For some, too much structure and support has already been provided, and we realize that they will never walk alone unless we remove some of those crippling crutches. For others—the "what-do-I-do-now"ers—we prop up the supports to insure some initial taste of success. These can be tossed away when they are no longer needed.

Our task is to guide and to tailor—but more importantly, to serve as models for our young. Research is on our side. Integrative teachers have produced integrative pupils. Dominative teachers have produced dominative pupils. Autonomous teachers should produce autonomous pupils. Is it worth a try?

Up to this point we have analyzed the notion of self-concept and broken it down into its four components: a sense of worth, a sense of coping, the ability to express feelings and emotions, and a sense of autonomy. All of these senses, which can be viewed as sub-selves, comprise our sense of self—our sense of self-identity. When we feel this sense of self-identity, we are identifying with our worth, our coping ability, our feelings and emotions, and our autonomy. How we feel about ourselves, in sum, is how we identify with our sub-selves.

The term *identify with* is the key to understanding our behavior. *What we identify with determines how we will behave.* If we identify with being a special person, we act like a special person. If we identify with being one who is loved, we act lovable. If we identify with successful coping, we cope successfully. If we feel good and accepting of our feelings and emotions, we monitor ourselves, we reduce our anxieties and frustrations when they occur, and we stay with ourselves. If we identify with autonomy, we behave autonomously. What we identify with is our own personal key to our behavior.

As teachers, this is our key to instruction. When, based on our observations, we are able to determine what the pupil identifies with, only then can we provide the experiences that enforce and reenforce the positive aspects and reduce, modify and change the negative aspects. How this is done is described later in this chapter and in Chapter 3. At this time it is important that we obtain another view of self-identity, of how it has and does relate to the individual in the context of a changing society.

The New Generation's Search for Role

Dr. William Glasser, in his book, *The Identity Society*,[2] has provided the kind of overview or gestalt that teachers and parents would find helpful in understanding how young people involved in a search for self-identity view this society and their relationship to it. His contribution is significant because of its immediate relevancy. For many he has removed the anxiety and guilt-ridden aspects of the "Where-Did-I-Go-Wrong?" syndrome.

Many of us in the sixties, functioning as teachers and as parents, were overwhelmed by the dramatic changes taking place in our young people. The disenchantment with education, the Viet Nam War and crises, the challenges directed at traditional value systems and at the Protestant work ethic, the new lifestyles, the increase in communes and the emergence of the "new" colleges were confronting us. All of these changes struck with the impact of a tornado. It appeared that our young people were turning the world upside down and inside out, and that we—autonomous as we were, skillful copers as we had been—were at a loss. To overreact would have been easy; to be able to act constructively required an understanding of the causes and the pattern of change. We knew what was happening but we couldn't fathom why it was happening. Viet Nam, affluence, permissiveness, political corruption, racism and compulsory miseducation were all tossed at us as possible causes. We could use any one or more and build a case. What we were looking at were isolated specifics, but what was needed was a systematic, cohesive explanation that was sound, credible, plausible, well-founded and well-grounded in reality, that we could understand and point to and say, "That's why!" The "That's why" is the substance of the first section of this chapter—the child's self-concept, his self-identity and his search for his identity in a world that had changed and was still in the flux of critical change.

"The times, they are a-changin'." In these times, priorities were changing and being reorganized. Many of us were blind to this, however; we were looking through the wrong glasses. The world in which many of us were raised was a goal-oriented and future-oriented world, a work-today, study-today and in-the-future-you-will-be-gratified world. In that world we strove for survival; our goals were survival goals. We were told that if we went to school and received a good education, we would obtain a good job, earn money and insure our survival. We were told that if we went to college, we would obtain a better job, earn more money and insure a better and longer survival.

Few of us thought or had the time to think of our identities, of who we really were or what we really felt or what we really valued. Our goal was not to determine our role as unique individuals. We were not searching for ourselves. We were searching for a goal—an occupation, a career, a means to survive in society. We would become teachers, businessmen, lawyers, doctors, nurses, secretaries or farmers first. This was our priority. We would have extrinsic value. After we had attained this goal, we would focus on the self. That was the way many of us did it. That was the way it had always been and would always be. Was there any other way? Goal first, role second—if we got around to it.

But the young people brought up in the society of the fifties and sixties did not see it that way. Our society had established and secured survival mechanisms. Few people starved. Unemployment insurance, social security and the welfare system insured some measure of survival. One could make it. The priorities were reversed. Role first, then goal. I want to find myself first; I want to be me first.

To many of the young, the flourishing society was viewed as mechanistic and materialistic, preaching ersatz values and practicing other values. Inner happiness rarely appeared and hypocrisy was evident. Whether we view these young as idealists, rebels, prophets of the future or nonconformists is insignificant. They are the products of their times, as we were the products of our times. As the times change, priorities again will be reorganized. Values and lifestyles again will change. What is crucial is that we understand and we accept the realities of this process and that we educate for it.

Our schools cannot ignore the role-oriented youth anymore than we can ignore the goal-oriented youth. Our task is not judgmental in nature. Within a modified framework, our schools can instruct for both role and goal. There is no conflict. We are individuals: we have roles and identities. We are also valuable individuals to society: we have goals. To be fully functioning, both are essential for role and goal reinforce each other. They are not distinct entities; they are parts of a whole.

In the past our schools have dealt primarily with one—with

goal. In the present and the future we must deal with both. Is there another way? We really can't be certain of that, can we?

Creating a Responsive Environment

Viewing self-identity as a relevant goal of our schools, just how do we begin? We begin by creating a responsive environment, one that is responsive to free and open communication and facilitates a maximum of interaction. The environment, to a very large extent, will determine our success.

First, we must create an open climate. By our verbal directions, voice, tone and body language, we communicate this feeling of openness. The pupil should be made to feel that he is free to speak about his feelings, thoughts and experiences, and that his inputs and responses are welcome.

Second, we must establish a climate that is accepting. The pupil should be made to feel that his feelings, thoughts and experiences are accepted nonjudgmentally. One's feelings are personal realities: they are neither right nor wrong, good nor bad. We do not judge, evaluate, criticize or deprecate them. We talk about, share and accept them. We are honest about them.

Third, the climate must be one that is clarifying. We not only express our feelings, thoughts and experiences—we develop, expand, analyze and attempt to understand them in the context in which they occurred. What happened? What conditions prompted these feelings? If conditions had been different would we have felt the same way? Could we have changed the conditions? How? Would different individuals have reacted in different ways? Why?

Fourth, the climate must provide for interaction. The pupils should feel free to share; to hitchhike on each others experiences; to make comparisons by identifying similarities, commonalities and differences, and to discuss possible consequences and the effects of these consequences on future behaviors.

To maximize interaction, the physical arrangement of the pupils must be considered. Pupils seated in rows or at separate tables scattered about the room have difficulty in communicating freely. Pupils should be seated in a circular or U shaped arrangement. This enables all pupils to face each other and stimulates interaction. The pattern of interaction should not be restricted from teacher to pupil and back to teacher. The pattern may begin with the teacher and then move on to many pupils, fostering a great deal of pupil-pupil discussion.

I can recall an occasion in which the staff of a school, recognizing the importance of creating a responsive environment, decided to concentrate on the first four factors with which I have just dealt. They decided to use videotapes to assess the degree to which they had created an open, accepting, clarifying and interactive climate. I served as director of instruction in this program. As I was leaving the school, one of the teachers asked me if I would stop and view a ten-minute videotape she had just made. She was concerned about one pupil's performance on the tape. I consented. The technique being used was microteaching. The teacher had six pupils around a table engaged in a discussion.

On the tape, I watched the teacher direct her opening question at this pupil. The repetitive interaction was teacher to pupil, teacher to pupil. The teacher asked what had happened in regard to a personal incident the pupil had mentioned. The pupil responded enthusiastically. The teacher asked where it had happened. The pupil responded and shifted about in his chair. The teacher asked the pupil if he were certain of his information. The pupil responded and moved his chair away from the table. The teacher asked about the conditions and circumstances of the incident. The pupil responded uneasily and with some reluctance. The deluge of questions continued until the pupil's responses were monosyllabic. The tape was over.

"Well, what do you think was wrong with him?" she asked. I smiled. "You are really gung ho on creating the proper kind of climate. You are definitely determined. I want you to play the tape back for yourself once more before you erase it. But as you play it back, focus on the affective climate you are creating."

"You are asking the right questions, but reassess the tone of your voice, your body language and your facial expressions. You so desperately want to help this pupil. Picture yourself as the pupil and assess how you would react. Are you trying too hard? Are you coming across too strong?"

She was so intent on creating the proper climate that her tone, voice, body language and facial expressions had an inhibiting effect on the pupil.

A few weeks later the teacher called me. "Come in and see the new tapes: same teacher, same pupils, same questions, but what a difference!" She was right. She was relaxed, warm, friendly, smiling, accepting and clarifying. She was letting it happen—not forcing it to happen. What a difference!

"Muriel, how did you sense what was happening?" she asked.

I smiled. "The same thing happened to me! When I asked a colleague to assess my early tapes, I was instructed to view my behaviors and associate with the Spanish Inquisition! The message was loud and clear. In fact, I was told rather bluntly that I was using an 'attack and defend' strategy. The pupils were viewing my questions, as they were delivered, as personal attacks, and they proceeded to defend themselves at first and then gradually retreated. The words 'attack and defend' strategy had made their impact on me. I became keenly aware that if I sought authentic communication and interaction, the affective delivery was as crucial as the cognitive structure of the questions."

Since relevant discussion and interaction depend upon active listening, the fifth factor essential in establishing this climate is the promotion of listening skills. Pupils should be impressed with the fact that we listen to each other; we do not focus on what we are preparing to say. We focus on the speaker; only then do we become truly involved, and only then can we really respond in a meaningful way.

The Self-Fulfilling Prophecy in Operation

Sixth, and most important, is the teacher's expectations of individual pupils. How the teacher views his or her role in these encounters, how the teacher perceives the participants, what his or her expectations are in each situation, are communicated to the pupils. Our self-fulfilling prophecies somehow come to be realized. The study conducted by Rosenthal and Jacobson indicate that this may be case.[3] The central concept behind their investigation was that of the self-fulfilling prophecy. "The essence of this concept is that one person's prediction of another person's behavior becomes a reality."

Dr. Rosenthal administered a new intelligence test to all children in a particular elementary school. He then informed the teachers that based on "obtained" results specific pupils would demonstrate significant gains in academic achievement and could be viewed as potential academic "spurters." The data given to the teachers were false. The children who were designated as "spurters" were randomly selected. What was startling was that children from whom teachers expected greater intellectual gains did indeed demonstrate these gains.

In addition, it was extremely interesting to note how the teachers perceived these "spurters." When asked to describe these children, the teachers stated that "they were more curious, more interesting, alive and more autonomous learners and had a better chance of experiencing happiness and success in later life than did their peers."

3. Robert Rosenthal and Lenore F. Jacobson, "Teacher Expectations for the Disadvantaged", Scientific American, Vol. 218, No. 4, April 1968, pp. 19-23.

Essentially what Rosenthal had succeeded in doing was to establish rather glowing teacher expectations which obviously had some effects upon the teachers' behavior, which in turn promoted pupil learning. Rosenthal had hypothesized that the teacher expectations may have been communicated by the teacher's tone of voice, facial expressions, or posture and this in effect somehow enhanced the child's self-concept, level of motivation and cognitive skills. Although further research will be needed to test this hypothesis, it appears that the "self-fulfilling prophecy" does operate.

Therefore, in dealing with our teaching role in creating an environment responsive to communication, we must be wary of those halos we toss about and the hypothetical expectations we establish for our children, and keenly observe what does occur. We must then modify our expectations based on our observations.

In addition to being cognizant of our expectations, we must, at all times demonstrate authentic behavior. Just as we expect our children to be themselves, we in turn must be ourselves. Children have an uncanny sense of recognizing when you are you and when you are not. If teacher behavior is not authentic, the entire process becomes a sham.

In sum, the climate which we create must be characterized by being open, accepting, clarifying, fostering interaction and listening skills, and guided by our authentic actions and realistic expectations.

How to Use the
Behavioral Outcomes Approach to
Promote a Positive Self-Concept
in Pupils

Having created the climate conducive to communication, we are now concerned with the process skills and strategies to promote a strong and positive self-concept. Our task is to provide ample and relevant opportunities to enable the pupil to get in touch with his feelings, express, accept, clarify and understand them. Only by doing so can he monitor himself and be motivated to take constructive action toward the enhancement of his sense of self-worth, coping and autonomy.

The focus of all of our procedures is on the expression and processing of feelings and emotions and the behaviors which they elicit. The key term is processing. Our approach is the Behavioral Outcomes Approach. The central theme of my book, *Effective*

Teaching Strategies With the Behavioral Outcomes Approach[4] was directed at using process skills in the cognitive domain. The unanticipated and outstanding success of this approach prompted me to write the book. What better reason to put it in a book!

The approach has worked with all kinds of children at all grade levels. Teachers developed comptetency with the approach and were enthusiastic, and pupils demonstrated successful achievement. But what was unanticipated were the affective gains of the approach. Children who had been "turned off" by learning were "turned on." Motivation, involvement and feelings of self-worth, coping and autonomy were strengthened. Why these affective gains? They were byproducts. Couldn't we convert them into products?

The answer was staring us in the face. We were using process skills, applying them to the cognitive domain. Why not apply them to the whole child—to the affective domain as well? The content we were processing was the content of the disciplines; why not focus on the content of the individual or of the person: his feelings, emotions, beliefs, attitudes, interests and appreciations. What could be more relevant? We had labeled these skills cognitive skills and in so doing we had looked upon them purely as skills or processes which could be applied solely to the cognitive domain. This was where we had gone wrong—but only partially wrong. These process skills had to be applied to both domains and both types of content: person content and that of the disciplines. The Behavioral Outcomes Approach had to be expanded.

As a consultant to numerous school systems which were implementing the approach based on its initial demonstrated success, the movement into the affective domain was welcomed and the results were evident. Based on teacher observations, pupils demonstrated significant growth in self-concept and in intrinsic motivation, discipline problems were reduced and pupil achievement and affective growth increased.

Our task now is to become thoroughly acquainted with these process skills, so that they are internalized, become "intuitive" and are readily applicable to the classroom. In Chapter 3 and in those which follow, you will be on the two-lane highway. The signposts are clearly marked *role* and *goal*, and eventually the lanes merge. Our destination is the development of the whole individual.

---

4. Muriel Gerhard *Effective Teaching Strategies with the Behavioral Outcomes Approach.* West Nyack, N.Y.: Parker Publishing Company, Inc., 1971.

3

How to "Process"
for
Affective Learning

Having been provided with a specific and detailed concept of self-image and an affective description of the search for self-identity and the need for role development, we are ready to move ahead.

In this chapter and those which follow you are presented with:

- A listing of the process skills to promote affective learning so that you have an overview of the skills in which you will develop competency.

- Operational definitions of each process skill so that you know precisely what to do when you are using each process.

- The rationale for applying each process in an affective context.

- Sample questions and specific strategies for each process for direct application.

- Samples of relevant content—"person" content as well as "curricular" content.

- Summary charts of the process skills and their affective application to "person" and "curricular" content.

In sum, the following chapters will provide you with the process skills and resources to promote affective growth. As you review the process skills which follow, keep in mind that the operational definitions are stated in the *context of the affective domain*. They are applied to the cognitive domain when they are useful and relevant to the clarification of feelings, emotions, attitudes, beliefs, values and behaviors. As has been stated previously, both *cognitive and affective learning are crucial to complete learning*. Our purpose here and now is to promote and strengthen the affective dimension of learning in our schools and to enhance cognitive learning by developing a strong and positive self-image in our pupils.

A Listing of Process Skills for Affective Learning

Process	*Operational Definition*
1. Observing	Describing what is observed and heard; identifying the facts.
2. Associating	The instant recalling of feelings, emotions, behaviors, events, objects and thoughts as they come to mind.
a. Free Association	The instant recalling of feelings, emotions, behaviors, events, objects and thoughts as they come to mind with *no restrictions imposed.*
b. Controlled Association	The instant recalling of feelings, emotions, behaviors, events, objects and thoughts as they come to mind but restricted to a given context or area of concern.
c. Linked Association	The instant recalling of feelings, emotions, behaviors, events, objects and thoughts as they come to mind, in which each association becomes the stimulus word for the next association, resulting in a train of associations; i.e., yellow—sun—vacation—good times.
3. Comparing	Identifying similarities and differences; the data may consist of facts, thoughts, feelings, beliefs, attitudes, values and behaviors.
4. Classifying	Establishing an arbitrary system of groupings on the basis of the common *affective* characteristics that the elements engender in us; i.e., things I value, things I do not value; issues I feel strongly about, issues I readily dismiss.
5. Analyzing	Breaking down a problem, situation or behavior into its component parts in terms of thoughts, feelings, beliefs and values so that relationships and interrelationships are made explicit; order-

ing the component parts so that the relative hierarchy of ideas or values are made clear.

6. Interpreting

Expressing the personal meaning of an experience or body of data, constructing inferences and making predictions.

7. Generalizing

Using specific situations or phenomena, comparing them and arriving at patterns, principles or rules affecting behavior.

8. Divergent Thinking

Offering various options, choices, alternative patterns or solutions to the same problem or situation.

9. Critical Thinking

Analyzing situations or bodies of data to determine relationships, evaluating the situation or data by weighing the negative and positive components for the purpose of making a decision.

10. Creative Thinking

Using feelings, emotions, ideas, words, objects, etc., developing them, organizing and reorganizing them and arriving at a solution or product which is novel, original or unexpected in its new form.

11. Concept Formation

Arriving at a broad understanding by comparing, analyzing and classifying data and abstracting and generalizing its meaning so that it is applicable to new situations.

In addition to the listing of process skills to promote affective learning, it is essential that we define the key terms which we are using throughout this book. The purpose is evident—so that you understand these terms as I understand them.

Key Terminology

Terms	Definitions
Feelings	Reactions to experiences expressed as mild emotions ranging from pleasantness to unpleasantness; may be viewed as the overtone or the coloring of an experience serving as the self-evaluating aspect of our adjustment to the environment.

Emotions	Strong bodily reactions varying in intensity and impelling us to action.
Beliefs	Propositions or doctrines which are emotionally accepted on the basis of what we implicitly consider adequate grounds. (The grounds for belief, however, are often not examined, nor does the believer imply that others need have the same grounds.) Beliefs have varying degrees of subjective certitude.
Attitudes	Learned predispositions to behave in a consistent way toward a given class of objects, people, situations, not as they are, but as they are conceived to be. It is by the *consistency of response* to a situation, a class of objects, people that an attitude is identified. This predisposition to behave has a directive effect upon feelings and action related to the person or object.
Values	Traits, objects, goals that have *great personal worth,* that are prized and cherished.
Value System	A more or less coherent set of values that regulate a person's conduct, often without his awareness that they do so. An individual's own value system may be at variance with the value system of a social group resulting in a conflict of values. One's public values may not be congruent with one's private values.
Behavior	Any action, reaction or interaction on the part of an individual. The behavior may be overt (readily observable) or covert (hidden and not easily detectable). Behavior is not viewed as *solely observable action:* both overt and covert actions are encompassed in our definition.

The Three Levels of Operation:
Feeling, Thought and Action

Equipped with the listing of process skills and brief descriptions of their operational definitions, which are expanded as we deal with each process, we are ready to explore each process and become thoroughly acquainted with the questioning techniques and specific strategies. In using these questioning techniques and strategies, we are operating on three levels—the affective level (feelings, beliefs, values), the thinking level and the action or behavioral level. We want the pupil to become keenly aware of his feelings, beliefs, attitudes and values, to understand his thoughts and his actions as they *directly relate* to these affective components and to be able to express these relationships and interrelationships in a coherent manner.

Selecting Affective Content

The sources of content which we use in operating on these three levels are: the person, namely the individual himself—his feelings, beliefs, attitudes, values, thoughts and his experiential background; the "outside" curriculum, namely the content gleaned from the media—television, motion pictures, radio, newspapers, magazines, books, and the "school" curriculum, the content of the disciplines—materials from language arts, social studies, music, art, the sciences, etc.

The kind of content which you select to use initially will depend on the kinds of pupils you have. Some teachers have found that using "person" content first is extremely stimulating. What could be more relevant than for pupils to deal with their own world and concerns! Having worked with "person" content first, pupils find the "discipline" content relevant. They seem to transfer the relevancy from one to the other. On the other hand, some teachers have found that pupils are threatened by a direct approach. Pupils prefer to deal with experiences which have been encountered by someone they know or someone they read about. In this case, teachers utilize the "outside" content or the "discipline" content first and gradually make the transition to "person" content. The choice rests with the teacher. Either approach is effective as long as the content selected is not trite or artificial, pupils identify with it and it reflects their concerns.

Developing Process Skills

As you review each process skill, you will find for each an expanded operational definition, the questioning techniques, and the specific strategies which may be readily applied in your classroom.

Observing

We are starting with the process of observation. The rationale is evident: if our pupils are to be involved in affective processing and clarification they must operate from *the base of reality*. The skills of observation are essential to determine this base or to get as close to it as possible. Observation is our primary way of knowing: since it is our firsthand method of learning, it is a skill we cannot ignore.

An Operational Definition: When we are observing we are using all of our five senses in order to maintain close and continuous contact with reality. For our purposes we have limited *observation* to two processes, those of observing and listening. This may sound redundant; an explanation is in order. We could have used the terms seeing and hearing, but these are biological processes that requires no training. However, both observing and listening are psychological processes that are learned. These are the processes which we are attempting to develop in our pupils.

We begin by focusing on questions such as: What are we observing? What is really going on out there? Are we observing the total scene? Are we observing only what we want to observe? Are we observing more than what is actually out there? Do we have any "blind spots"? Do others observe what we observe? Are we listening? What are we receiving? Are we receiving what we want to receive? Are we tuning out at times? Can we report accurately what was said? Are we interpreting what was said? Are our own biases distorting what we "see" and "hear"?

The Filters and Screens of Observation

Observation is by no means a simple process. The factors which limit and distort observation are many. Our own experiences clearly bear this out. We have learned, in many instances, to observe and listen selectively and screen out unpleasant or disturbing sights and sounds. Our past experiences, beliefs, attitudes, values, goals, and interests all serve as filters. The observations we and others make tell us a great deal about ourselves and others.

A workshop on human relations comes to mind. At this workshop, a variety of transparencies were flashed across the screen. One transparency consisted of two houses in the suburbs, a moving van, two white adults, two black youngsters and two white youngsters. One of the white youngsters was holding a bat and a ball.

The workshop participants were asked to describe what they saw. Responses such as the following were given. "The black children are moving into the neighborhood. They want to play with the white children who are reluctant to play with them." "The white adults are watching a black family move into their neighborhood and are very distraught." What was observable were—two houses, one moving van, two white adults, two black youngsters and two white youngsters, a bat and a ball—but what was "seen" were the biases of a number of people, distorting the actual picture.

As was stated previously, observation is a learned process. As teachers we should provide pupils with ample opportunities to develop this process. Pupils who are keen observers and attentive listeners are able to obtain accurate and comprehensive information to confront and react to the real world in a meaningful manner. The process of observation is basic to all other processes presented in this book. It is essential to both cognitive and affective development— whether we are dealing with knowledge of the desciplines or knowledge of the self, *our base must be factual reality*.

Structuring Questions for Observation

The process of structuring questions for observation are effortless! The questions are basic:

- Name what you have observed.
- Describe what you have observed.
- Describe all of your observations in regard to a static object.
- Describe the behavior or interaction between or among the individuals you observed.
- Describe the event.
- Record as accurately as you can what you have observed.
- Write a report on what you have observed.
- Describe what you have "heard."
- Record the conversation which you have "heard."
- Having witnessed the situation, describe in as factual a way as you can, what you have observed and what you have heard.

Strategies for Promoting Observation

The strategies for observation are as basic as the questions. Their application is effortless for the teacher; their use is an eye-opener for the pupils. Pupils are constantly astounded at what they failed to observe and the variations in the observations of their classmates. Promoting observation is never dull!

- Given a picture, photograph, transparency, drawing, etc., *name* all the things you have observed.

- Given a picture, photograph, etc., of a person(s), place or object(s) *describe in detail* what you have observed.

- Given a situation in which people are interacting, *describe all aspects of the interaction.*

- Given a segment of a film, describe what you observed and heard.

- Given a role-playing situation, describe what actually occurred.

- Having taken a trip to _____, report on the trip; describe the sights and sounds of the trip as well as the events.

- Having listened to a record or a tape, describe what you "heard."

- Having listened to a speech, a T.V. commentator or a talk show, give as factual a report as possible on all that was communicated.

- Having heard a story or a play, describe the characters and their behaviors.

- Given a "surprise" situation which was enacted by a group of pupils, write an account of what actually occurred.

- Compare your reported observations with those of your classmates. How were they similar? How were they different? Which of the observations were highly accurate? Which of the observations were interpretations of the information? Which of the observations were inferences or explanations of what had occurred, as opposed to what did occur?

Content for Observation

The content for observation is all around us, from the chalk on the blackboard to the actual interactions in the room. I am reminded of the story of the professor who wanted to get his pupils to realize that they were extremely poor observers. He proceeded to do so by hanging a sheet of white paper on the blackboard. He then placed a black dot on the center of the paper. "What do you observe?" he asked his students. They all laughed. "The black dot, of course!" was the response. All had ignored the paper!

In sum, I don't believe that we will ignore the paper. The following list is by no means exhaustive. I am certain that the lists you compile as you "process" with observation will be extensive.

A Listing of Sample Content for Observation

Objects in the classroom
The school building
The school environment
People
People working
People playing
People communicating
Animals
Pet behavior
Trees, plants, flowers, plant growth
Changing seasons
Forms of precipitation
Science demonstrations
Machines, gadgets, utensils
Art, paintings, sculpture
Music, songs, records, tapes
News, speeches, television reporters
Favorite television shows
Readings of stories, plays, poems, articles
Films, filmstrips, videotapes

Associating

Provided with a means of obtaining a factual base, we now move ahead to our affective exploration.

An operational definition: When we are associating, we are freely recalling our feelings, emotions, thoughts and experiences as they relate directly to a stimulus. The stimulus may be a feeling, thought, specific behavior, specific event, person, place or object. Our reaction is instantaneous and spontaneous. We do not ponder; we simply express our reactions as we recall them.

Kinds of Association

We may use various kinds of association. These include free controlled and linked association. Let's begin with free association.

When we associate freely with a feeling, concept, behavior, event or person, we express all of the things that come to mind. The world is our domain. Anything goes: there are no limits or restrictions. We are given an initial stimulus which denotes a feeling, concept, behavior, event, person or object, and are asked to respond.

Let's illustrate this. Suppose you are given the stimulus word *friendly*. *When you feel friendly, what do you think of?* The responses may be: "When I feel friendly, I think of going to parties with my friends, sharing things with others, talking and laughing with people, caring about people, doing things with my family, doing things for people, going on a picnic, etc." You could go on and on recalling friendly faces, people, events, stories, plays, works of art, music, etc. You have the whole world with which to associate.

Now let's use controlled association. In controlled association, we place limits or restrictions on the area in which we operate. We define the parameters within which the associations take place.

For example, we may give the pupil the stimulus word *school* and ask him: *When you think of school, what kinds of feelings do you experience?* Here we are limiting him to the school environment. We may restrict his area of operation still further. *When you think of reading in school, what kinds of feelings do you experience? When you think of your family, what kinds of feelings do you experience? When you think of your brother or sister or father or mother, what kinds of feelings do you experience?* The degree to which we control the associations depends on our specific purposes. In some instances, controlled association is a more efficient tool. We know the area of concern which we wish to explore, and we focus on it. In other instances, exploring a large area is essential in order to pinpoint the specific area of major concern.

The third type of association is linked association. When we are using linked association, we use a variety of stimulus words or phrases. However, we have no control over these stimuli other than providing the initial one. The individual carries on from there. Each thought or feeling generated serves as the stimulus for the next thought or feeling. For example, let's use *boredom* as the initial stimulus. *When you feel bored, what do you think of? What other feelings do you experience?* As you analyze this sequence, note how each word or words becomes the stimulus for the succeeding one. The individual is instructed not to return the word "boredom", but to use each link in the chain to determine the next link. The sequence may be: When I think of "boredom," it reminds me of someone doing nothing, which reminds me of feeling blue, which conjures up blue skies, which are reflected in blue waters, which reminds me of fish, which reminds me of the T.V. commercial for Arthur Treacher's. The fact that we started with the feeling of boredom and ended up with Arthur Treacher's is not of major significance. Going to Arthur Treacher's for fish may reduce boredom, but that is not the point at this moment.

Association as a Dual Tool

What *is* the point is that the association techniques are useful tools for recalling our experiences and their attendant feelings, thoughts and emotions, expressing them and becoming aware of them. We are simultaneously exploring our cognitive and affective memory banks, sorting out and clarifying our thoughts, feelings and behaviors. Association is a creative vehicle for opening up this storehouse of experience and demonstrating the relationships between thoughts and feelings. It is analogous to brainstorming our selves.

When we use free association, we obtain a very general but useful profile of the pupil. When we use controlled association, our map is restricted to a region and the profile we obtain is more specific and detailed. When we use linked association, we find ourselves involved in a stream of consciousness which provides unusual insights for both pupils and teachers.

Effects of Affective Association on Pupils and Teachers

Pupil reaction to association is surprising. Teachers feel as if they had just discovered a hidden latch or button which triggers unusual involvement. Pupils attend, respond, free-wheel and interact. Since there are no right or wrong answers, the threat of making a mistake or of being evaluated or judged is removed. The classroom comes alive. Pupils who normally retreated or responded only when called upon are volunteering to participate. The problem is not one of stimulating involvement but of distributing the time so that all may participate.

In sum, pupils, in becoming active participants, become more confident about themselves and in their ability to get in touch with their feelings, emotions, beliefs, values and to express them; teachers obtain a broader view of their pupils and become more understanding and empathic, for they are entering into the feelings, beliefs and values of their pupils as well as into their ideas. Bill, John and Nancy are no longer viewed as good students, poor, average or excellent students, but are seen as persons in their own right—as unique individuals.

Structuring Questions for General Association

The process of structuring questions to promote association requires little effort. Questions such as the following are used on a general level:

- What comes to mind when you think of _____?
- List all the things, people or events that you associate with _____.
- When X occurs, what do you think of?
- When you heard about _____ what did you recall?
- When you observe _____ what does it remind you of?

Structuring Questions for Affective Association

Questions such as the following are used on the affective level:

- When you feel _____ (sad, worried, etc.), what comes to mind?
- When you think of being _____ (liked, disliked, friendly, etc.), what comes to mind?
- When you have to _____ (make a choice, settle an argument, handle a tough situation, etc.), how do you feel?
- When you _____ (do a good job, mess things up, fail, etc.), how do you feel?

Fifty Association Questions to Promote Self-Concept for Direct Classroom Use

1. When you think of someone being a unique individual, what characteristics do you think of?
2. When you think of being yourself, what characteristics do you think of?
3. When you think of being special, what comes to mind?
4. When you think of special people, who do you think of?
5. When you feel special, what feelings do you have?
6. When you feel different, what comes to mind?

7. When you think of being friendly, what things do you do?

8. When you think of being liked, what things or events come to mind?

9. When you think of being disliked, what things or events come to mind?

10. When you think of being disliked, what feelings do you have?

11. When you think of someone you like, what things do you like about him or her?

12. When you think of someone you dislike, what things annoy you about him or her?

13. When you think of your friends in school, how do you feel?

14. When you think of your friends outside of school, how do you feel?

15. When someone chooses you to help them, how do you feel?

16. When someone chooses someone else instead of you, how do you feel?

17. When you do a good job how do you feel?

18. When you can't handle a situation, how do you feel?

19. When you have to ask for help, how do you feel?

20. When you are asked to help someone, how do you feel?

21. When you have to make choices that are important to you, how do you feel?

22. When you think of your family, what things come to mind?

23. When you think of the happy times you spent with your family, what do you remember?

24. When you think of spending time at home with your family, what feelings do you have?

25. When you think of what your parents expect of you, what comes to mind?

26. When you think of what your parents expect of you, what feelings do you experience?

27. When you think of school, what comes to mind?

28. When you think of the things you enjoy in school, what comes to mind?

29. When you think of the things you dislike in school, what comes to mind?

30. When you think of things which upset you in school, what comes to mind?

31. When you think of your best subjects, what comes to mind?

32. When you think of some of your favorite teachers, what are some of the things about them that made them special?

33. When you think of things you enjoy doing, what comes to mind?

34. When you think of places you would like to go to, what comes to mind?

35. When you think of your favorite songs, what comes to mind?

36. When you think of books you enjoyed reading, what comes to mind?

37. When you think of people you really admire and would like to be like, what comes to mind?

38. When you feel happy, what comes to mind?

39. When you feel sad, what comes to mind?

40. When you feel angry, what comes to mind?

41. When you feel worried, what comes to mind?

42. When you feel frightened, what comes to mind?

43. When you feel disappointed, what do you do?

44. When you feel no one cares, what do you do?

45. When you feel unsure of yourself, what do you do?

46. When people criticize you, how do you feel? What do you do?

47. When you are praised, how do you feel?

48. When you have to deal with people younger than you, how do you feel? What do you do?

49. When you have to deal with people older than you, how do you feel? What do you do?

50. When people express beliefs that are different from yours, how do you feel? What do you do?

The preceeding 50 sample association questions deal with the development of the self-concept. Since our self-concept is a function of how we perceive ourselves and how others perceive, interact with and react to us, the intrinsic value of these questions and the relevant "person" content they incorporate is obvious.

Strategies for Affective Association

Strategy #1—Associating with Feelings and Thoughts

Basic Structures:

- How would you feel if _____ the following occurred?
- Why do you think you would feel this way?

Strategy #2—Associating with Feelings, Thoughts and Behaviors[1]

Basic Structures:

- Let's explore an incident that occurred that was significant to you, someone you know or someone you read about, or something you saw on T.V. *or:* let's explore a story, poem, play, song or film which we have experienced in class.
- Tell us what happened.
- How did you feel about it? What feelings did you experience?
- How do you think the other people involved in the happening felt?
- What did you do or what do you think you would have done?
- How did you feel then or how do you think you would have felt?
- What did the other people do in this situation?
- How do you think they felt then?

In using these questions, allow as many pupils as possible to provide their inputs in terms of how they would have felt, what they would have done and how they would have felt as a result of their actions. All too soon pupils will realize how differently people will respond in certain situations and how similar the feelings and actions will be in other situations.

Using Person Content—A Classroom Experience

Let's apply Strategy #2 to a personal incident. Ralph, who is in the seventh grade, tells the class that he had come home with his report card and had received B's in his major subject and C's in his minor subjects. His parents really "hassled" him. "How come he had received B's? He could do much better! How would he get into a 'good' college when the competition was so stiff? His sister had made all A's! Why didn't he work harder? He had no right to watch so much television. He should be hitting his books. Some changes had to be made!"

Ralph expressed his feelings. He was confused; he felt angry. He thought he had done his best, and felt resentment toward his parents, even toward his sister. He really didn't know if he wanted to go to college, but was afraid to voice this. He felt B's were fine, and didn't want to be compared with his sister.

1. Dr. Norman E. Wallen et. al., Final Report on the TABA Curriculum Development Project in Social Studies, Grades one through eight. San Francisco State College, October 1969, Project No. 5-1314, Grant No. OE-6-10-182. U.S. Department of Health, Education and Welfare, page 27.

Other pupils expressed similar incidents. Some felt that their parents were right because they themselves felt they could do better, that they were just coasting along. One youngster told about a beating he had received. His reaction was that "he was no good." His father wouldn't really beat him up because of a mark. His father beat him up because he was "no good."

Other students pointed out that getting poor grades didn't mean you were "no good." Surely you could feel "no good" becuase you failed, but you shouldn't feel "no good" all over.

In exploring how he thought his parents felt, Ralph felt they were disappointed and sad, but that they really cared about him. They really wanted the best for him because they loved him.

The discussion continued in terms of what Ralph did and what other pupils had done in similar situations. No, we did not solve Ralph's problem, nor did we attempt to. This was not our objective. But what was achieved was extremely significant. Feelings and emotions were expressed, exchanged freely and clarified. Ralph didn't feel that he was the only one in a leaky boat. He hadn't really thought about how his parents felt. "I guess parents want the best for their kids and sometimes they just push too hard. They really care about me." The overall feeling about the situation appeared to lose its intensity. The feelings were expressed and accepted.

This is but one sample of the use of "person" content. A complete volume could be written dealing with the many personal concerns of our pupils, but space prohibits this.

Applying an Association Strategy to "Curricular" Content

Let us apply association strategy #2 to a poem we might read in class at the elementary level. We are using the poem as a vehicle to assist the pupil in exploring *his feelings about himself and others.*

*Nobody
Loves Me*[2]

Somedays,
nobody loves me
so I go down the names
I know:
   I hate Martha
   I hate James

2. "Nobody Loves Me" from *All That Sunlight* by Charlotte Zolotow. Text copyright © 1967 by Charlotte Zolotow. Reprinted by permission of Harper & Row, Publishers, Inc.

I hate Selma
I hate Jo.
Nobody likes me,
that I know.
Somedays,
everyone loves me
So I go down the names
I know:
    I love Martha
    I love James
    I love Selma
    I love Jo.
Everyone loves me
I know so!

                    Charlotte Zolotow

Application of Strategy #2

- Let's explore the poem.
- Tell us what happened.
- How do you think the writer feels?
- Because the writer feels this way, how does he or she think others feel?
- What happens when the writer's feelings change?
- Have you ever felt this way?
- What happened?
- What did you do?
- How did you feel then?
- Do you know of other people who felt this way?
- What happened?
- What did they do?
- How did they feel then?

Now, let's apply association strategy #2 to a poem we might use with secondary pupils. In this case the pupil will be exploring his *feelings of self and of coping.*

Still Here[3]

I've been scarred and battered.
My hopes the wind done scattered.

3. Langston Hughes, "Still Here" in *Selected Poems,* New York: Alfred A. Knopf, Inc., 1948.

Snow has friz me, sun has baked me.
Looks like between 'em
They done tried to make me
Stop laughin'! stop lovin'! stop livin'-
But I don't care!
I'm still here!

Langston Hughes

Application of Strategy #2

- What happened to the writer?
- How does he feel?
- Do you recall an incident in which someone you know or someone you read about felt this way?
- Tell us about it. What happened?
- What did they do?
- Have you ever felt this way?
- What happened?
- What did you do?
- How did you feel then?

Merely from the sample questions and sample applications provided, it is evident that the opportunities for using association to promote affective growth are tremendous. Pupils readily become involved in self-exploration. Your problem will not be in turning pupils on to the process but in turning them off!

In Summary

In this chapter, we were introduced to the process skills for affective learning. Operational definitions of the process skills were provided, as well as definitions of the key terms to be used throughout the book. The three levels of operation to be used in applying the process strategies were described, as well as the kinds of content which constitute our affective curriculum. The processes of observation and association were dealt with in detail, by providing the rationale for their use, structured questions, specific strategies and sample content for direct classroom use. In the following chapter we will deal with the process skills of comparing, classifying and analyzing, as they are applied directly to affective learning.

4 Expanding the Process Skills in the Affective Domain

In this chapter we are expanding our process skills. We are comparing, classifying and analyzing in the affective domain. As in the previous chapter, we are provided with detailed definitions of each process, the rationale for its use, structured questions, specific strategies, samples of the strategies applied to the "curricular" and "person" content for direct classroom use.

Comparing

An operational definition: When we are comparing, we are *identifying the similarities and differences* which exist based on our observations.

In dealing with the cognitive domain, the process is relatively simple. We merely describe people, places and things in terms of the properties they have in common and those in which they differ. For example, if we are comparing a glass with a cup we might state that they differ in size, shape, form, color and material, and that they are the same in terms of function.

In the affective domain, we are comparing feelings, emotions, beliefs, values and behaviors. We are comparing how we and others react to specific situations—by sharing the same feelings or displaying different ones. We are comparing how we and others may, in specific cases, share the same beliefs or differ in our beliefs. We are comparing how we and others, in given situations, demonstrate the same values or different values, and are discovering that these values, in turn, influence and determine diverse behaviors.

In the cognitive domain, the application of the process of comparison makes it equally apparent that there are both similarities and differences in our perceptions, thoughts, ideas and concepts.

The Rationale for Affective Comparison

The value of this process both affectively and cognitively is obvious. We are different yet the same. There is a commonality that binds us all, as well as distinct differences, which promote diversity and individuality. How we view these similarities and differences and how we feel about them will determine our behavior. Therefore, in our classrooms, it is essential that our pupils have ample opportunities to make these *affective comparisons,* to fully understand at gut level these differences and similarities, and to accept them, respect them and be able to deal with them effectively.

Structuring Questions for General Comparison

Based on our operational definition of comparison, the structuring of questions to promote this process is almost effortless. Questions such as the following are used:

- Compare two or more _____.
- Contrast _____ with _____.
- What are the significant similarities between _____ and _____?
- What are the significant differences between _____ and _____?
- Differentiate between _____ and _____.

Structuring Questions for Affective Comparison

Questions such as the following are used and these questions are the key questions in the strategies which follow:
Given a poem, short story, account, song, recording, etc:

- Compare your feelings with the writer's feelings. How are they similar? How are they different?
- Compare your beliefs with the writer's beliefs. How are they similar? How are they different?
- Compare your values with the writer's values. How are they similar? How are they different?
- Compare your actions, behaviors and experiences with the writer's actions or his proposed actions. How are they similar? How are they different?

Strategies for Making Affective Comparisons

The following four strategies are used for making comparisons in the affective domain. We are dealing with comparing feelings, emotions, beliefs, values and coping behaviors.

Strategy #1—Comparing Feelings

Basic Structures:

- Given a personal situation or story, play, poem, article, song, record, film, etc., describe what happened.
- How do you think X felt?
- Are there any clues to tell you why X felt that way? If yes, what are they?
- How do *you* feel about it?
- Why do you feel this way?
- Compare your feelings with X's feelings. How are they the same or different?
- Do you sympathize or empathize with X's feelings? Why or why not?

Strategy #2—Comparing Beliefs

Basic Structures:

- Given a personal situation, story, play, poem, article, record, song, film, etc., describe what happened.
- What does X believe, or what beliefs does X express?
- What clues do you have to tell you that this is so?
- What belief do *you* hold in this case? Why?
- In this case, what do you think most people would believe?
- Compare your belief with X's belief. How are they the same or different?
- Do you find it easy or difficult to understand and accept X's belief? Why?

Strategy #3—Comparing Values

Basic Structures:

- Given a personal situation, story, play, poem, article, record, song, etc., describe what happened.

- What did X do and or say?
- Why do you think X behaved in this way?
- Based on what X did and or said, what do you think he values?
- In this case, what would *you* value?
- Compare your values with X's values. In this case, are they the same or do they differ? How?
- Do you find it easy or difficult to understand and accept X's value? Why?

Strategy #4—Comparing Behaviors

Basic Structures:

- Given a personal situation, story, poem, play, article, film, etc., describe what happened.
- How did X feel?
- Why do you think X felt this way?
- What did X do?
- How would you have felt in this case?
- What would *you* have done? Why?
- Compare your behavior with X's behavior. Is it similar or different from his?
- Do you find it easy or difficult to understand and accept X's behavior? Why?

Applying the Comparison Strategies
to Curricular Content

Now let's apply a few of the comparison strategies to a poem we might use with elementary pupils. In this case the pupil will be comparing the writer's feelings, beliefs and values with his own. The poem, "Different," deals with feelings of self and others, and the belief that each of us has his or her own identify however different we are. The tone of the poem demonstrates that the writer values individuality.

Different[1]

Hey, hey! I'm just me!
I'm different from anyone else you'll see!
Taller than John—shorter than Sue—
Hair that is darker than Nancy's too—

1. Jo Carr, "Different," in Houghton Mifflin Reading Program, *Rewards,* Boston, Mass., Houghton Mifflin Company, 1974.

Eyes not black, nor really green,
Nor really blue, but in between.
I've got more freckles than Don or Ed,
And I'm not as strong as Billy or Fred.
Jane reads better, but I can add,
And Jim runs faster (which makes me sad!)
Johnny's arms are chocolate brown,
And he's got the happiest grin in town.
Judy's arms are almost white—
And I'm dark tan—and it's all all right,
'Cause Johnny is him, and I am me,
And Judy is Judy, plain to see,
And we're all as different as we can be!

Jo Carr

Strategy #1—Comparing Feelings

- Let's explore the poem "Different" by Jo Carr.
- What does the writer think of when she says that she is different from anyone else?
- How does she feel about being different?
- Are there any clues to tell you why she felt this way? If yes, what are they?
- How do *you* feel about being different?
- Do you think of yourself as being different? If so, how are you different?
- Are your feelings the same or different from the writer's? How are they the same or different?
- Do you sympathize or empathize with the writer's feelings? Why or why not?

Strategy #2—Comparing Beliefs

- Let's continue to explore the poem.
- Does the writer believe that people should be different? What clues do you have to tell you that this is her belief?
- What do *you* believe? If we are all different, do you feel we should be our different selves or try to be more like each other? Why?
- Do you think most people believe that each of us is different and should be different? What makes you think so?
- Is your belief the same or different from the writer's?
- Do you find it easy or difficult to understand and accept the writer's belief? Why?

Strategy #3—Comparing Values

- Let's continue to explore the poem.
- Just from reading the poem, do you think that the writer (values) wants very much to be her own self—to be as different as she is? Why?
- How strongly do *you* feel about being your own self? Does it matter *very much* to you, *just a little* or *not at all?* Why?
- Do you find it easy or difficult to understand and accept the writer's value? Why?

The poem has served as a vehicle enabling the pupils to compare their feelings, beliefs, values and proposed actions or behaviors with those of the writer. The process of comparison may be extended by having the pupils compare this poem with the others and identify similarities and differences among them. More importantly, the comparison of various pupils reactions to being different, to being proud of their differences provides the kinds of insights which are crucial to the development of a strong sense of one's identity. They have had the opportunity to explore and express what they feel, believe, value and would do—in essence, to express what they are.They have had the opportunity to listen to others express both similar and different feelings, beliefs, values and behaviors, enabling them to better understand others and become more accepting of these differences. If affective comparison achieves this, it has indeed achieved a great deal.

Classifying

An Operational Definition: When we are classifying, we are sorting "things," we are placing them into groups based on some criterion or group of criteria which *we have selected.* In the cognitive domain, we may do this readily by observing a group of objects, ideas, events, persons, etc., comparing them to elicit similarities and differences, and then based on the differences we select, we may establish a system of groups. The difference or differences we select become the criterion or criteria for our classification system. For example, pupils at the elementary level may be given a collection of buttons to classify. They may group them according to size, color, shape, number of holes, etc.—or they may use two or more criteria such as placing all large, red buttons in one group or all large, red, square buttons in one group.

In the affective domain, we are using classification to being affective order into our lives. Pupils are asked to establish their own classification systems based on the *common affective characteristics* that the elements, things, occurences engender in them. For example, let's return to the classification of buttons for a moment. I recall visiting a teacher in one of our schools who was focusing on classification in the cognitive domain. As I walked about and observed the different ways the pupils had grouped the buttons, I was totally perplexed by one youngster's groupings. Finally, I succumbed and asked, "How did you sort those buttons?" He stared at me for a moment and then smiled, "Oh, that was easy—those I like and those I don't like!"

In applying classification to the affective domain, we are classifying events, people, places, poems, stories, plays, songs, records, etc., in terms of *affective criteria*. Specifically if we use the area of feelings, we may classify any of the above in terms of: things I like or dislike, things which encourage or discourage me, things which make me feel autonomous or helpless, things which I fear or do not fear, and so on.

In terms of our beliefs, pupils have classified events, poems, songs, etc., as consonant with their beliefs, or disconsonant with them. Similarly in the area of values, criteria such as the following have been elicited from pupils: things I value or do not value; things I accept, reject or feel neutral about; things I would work for or exert little effort for, things I would give up valuable time for and things with which I wouldn't spend more than five minutes.

In the case of behaviors, criteria such as the following have been given: behaviors which I admire and those which I totally reject, behaviors which I would find difficult to deal with and those which I feel confident in tackling; behaviors which were harmful to others and those which were helpful to others.

Affective classification enables pupils to organize and reorganize their world in terms of criteria based on their current feelings, beliefs, values, attitudes and behavioral patterns. It enables them to analyze and synthesize *what is relevant to them.* I cannot help but wonder if there is any classification system which is of more personal value than this one?

Structuring Questions for General Classification

Questions such as the following are for general use:

- Into what kinds of groups can you place these items, objects, ideas, etc.?
- What characteristics or properties can you use to separate these items into groups?
- Using your own ideas, create your own grouping system and place these items into the groups.

Structuring Questions for Affective Classification

Questions such as the following are used in the affective domain: Given events, stories, poems, plays, essays, articles, songs, films, art works, issues, etc.,

- Place these into groups based on the feelings these experiences engender in you; e.g., those you enjoy or do not enjoy, those which interest you or do not interest you, those which you appreciate or do not appreciate, those you can readily identify with or those which bore you, etc.
- Place these into groups based on the beliefs these experiences reinforce weaken or contradict; e.g., those which reinforce your faith in democratic action and those which weaken this faith, those which reinforce your faith in people and those which weaken this faith, etc.
- Place these into groups based on the values these experiences reinforce, weaken, contradict or modify—namely, those which reinforce the things *you prize and cherish* and those which weaken them; e.g., those which reinforce your sense of self-worth or weaken it, those which reinforce your sense of autonomy or weaken it, those which reinforce your life goals or weaken them, etc.
- Place these into groups based on the behaviors or actions these experiences reinforce, weaken or modify; e.g., those which stimulate you to work for a cause, to volunteer time, effort, money, etc.

Strategies for Affective Classification

The following four strategies are used for applying classification to the affective domain. We are classifying by using criteria based on (a) feelings, (b) beliefs, (c) values, (d) behaviors.

Strategy #1—Classifying on the Basis of Feelings

Basic Structures:

- Given a variety of events, stories, plays, poems, songs, records, art forms, etc., or a mixture of these, review all of these.

- Compare them in terms of the kinds of feelings you experience as you read them or listen to them or observe them.
- Group them using any one or more of these feelings as criteria.
- Compare your grouping with those of your classmates. Discuss the similarities and differences in groupings.

Strategy #2—Classifying on the Basis of Beliefs

Basic Structures:

- Given a variety of events, stories, plays, poems, etc., or a mixture of these, review all of these.
- Compare them in terms of the beliefs they extol and those which you hold.
- Group them using any one or more of these beliefs as the criteria for classification.
- Compare your groupings with those of your classmates. Discuss the similarities and differences in the groupings.

Strategy #3—Classifying on the Basis of Values

Basic Structures:

- Given a variety of events, stories, plays, poems, etc., or a mixture of these, review all of them in terms of the values they reflect.
- Compare them in terms of the values they reflect and your own.
- Group them using any value or set of values as the criteria.
- Compare your groupings with those of your classmates. Discuss the similarities and differences in the groupings.

Strategy #4—Classifying on the Basis of Behaviors or Actions

Basic Structures:

- Given a variety of events, stories, plays, poems, etc., or a mixture of these, review all of these focusing on the behaviors or actions of the people involved.
- Compare their actions in response to the situations in which they found themselves.
- How would you have reacted in each of these situations?
- Group these using any criteria you would use in determining how one should act under these conditions.
- Compare your groupings with those of your classmates. Discuss the similarities and differences in the groupings.

Applying the Classification Strategies
to Curricular Content

In each of the four strategies, the basic pattern is the same. The pupil reviews the materials, identifies the writer's feelings, beliefs, values and behaviors, identifies his own, compares them with the writer's and then proceeds to group the materials on the basis of some criterion or criteria he or she selects. It is important to emphasize that the choice of criteria is the pupil's. If his feelings, beliefs, values and behaviors are consonant with the writer's, he may use these as the basis for classification; if they differ, he may select other criteria.

Let's illustrate the use of the classification strategies by applying them to curricular content, keeping in mind that the curricular content serves as an opener for dealing with personal content.

Applying Strategy #1—Classifying on the
Basis of Feelings

The variety of materials we are using consists of two poems, a song, a recording and an account of an individual's reaction to a critical situation.

Let's sing or listen to one stanza of Woody Guthrie's "This Land Is Your Land."

This Land Is Your Land[2]

This land is your land,
This land is my land,
From California—to the New York Island;
From the redwood forest—to the Gulf Stream
waters;
This land was made for you and me.

- What kinds of feelings do you experience when you first hear or sing this song? Does this song make you feel happy, sad, proud, disappointed?
- What kinds of things do you want to go out and do?
- How do you think the songwriter felt about this land?
- Do you feel the same way he does or differently? Why?

Let's read "I Will Not Forget."

2. "This Land Is Your Land," Words & music by Woody Guthrie. TRO- © Copyright 1956, 1958 — 1970 Ludlow Music, Inc., New York, N.Y. Used by permission.

I Will Not Forget

I will not forget my people.
I was born a Navajo, the Navajos are my people.
They have lost their land, their homes,
    their material possessions.
They have had hard years, dark years and sad
years
But they have not lost hope.
They started anew
They have shown me the way.
I will not lose hope.
I will not forget
I am proud to be a Navajo
I am—of my people.

- What kinds of feelings do you first experience when you read this poem?
- How do you feel when you think of your people?
- How does the writer feel about his people?
- Compare your feelings with the writer's. How are they the same? How are they different?

Let's read "Leaving."

Leaving

We are leaving
Leaving the land in which we were born
Leaving our homes, our people and
All that we hold so dear.

We are leaving
Leaving to build our lives once more
Leaving to become free
To find happiness in another land.

We are leaving
But will our land, our homes, our people
Ever leave us?

- What kinds of feelings do you first experience when you read this poem?
- How do you think the writer feels?
- Why do you think he feels this way?
- If you had to leave the land in which you were born, how do you think you would feel?

- Compare your feelings with the writer's feelings. How are they the same? How are they different?
- With what kinds of feelings are you left?

Let's explore the following account:

The policy of the United States Government has been to place Indians on reservations. This is an account of an Indian chief describing his struggle before being sent to a reservation:

I am tired of fighting. Our chiefs are killed . . . . The old men are all dead, It is cold and we have no blankets. The little children are freezing to death. My people, some of them have run away to the hills, and have no blankets, no food; no one knows where they are— perhaps freezing to death. I want to have time to look for my children and see how many of them I can find. Maybe I shall find them among the dead. Hear me, my chiefs! I am tired; my heart is sick and sad . . . . I will fight no more forever.

- What kinds of feelings do you experience when you read this account?
- How does the Indian chief feel?
- Why does he feel this way?
- Compare your feeling with the Indian chief's. How are they the same? How are they different?
- With what kinds of feelings are you left?

Listen to a recording of "Now That The Buffalo's Gone" made by Buffy Sainte-Marie, as she laments a people's loss and calls for assistance.

- What kinds of feelings do you experience when you hear the song?
- What is the songwriter telling us?
- How would you describe her feelings?
- If you were in her place, how would you feel?
- Compare your feelings with hers. How are they the same? How do they differ?
- With what kinds of feelings are you left?

Up to this point, pupils have experienced the materials, and identified and compared their feelings and the writer's feelings. Now pupils are asked to:

- Group these materials using any one or more of these feeling as criteria.

- Compare your groupings with those of your classmates. Discuss the similarities and differences in groupings.

Pupil Responses

Pupils' reactions in applying strategy #1 to these materials were very interesting. Most of them classified Woody Guthrie's song, "This Land Is My Land" as giving them a feeling of joy and pride. The poems, "I Will Not Forget" and "Leaving" were classified as engendering feelings of loss and sadness. Some pupils included the Indian chief's lament in this group. Others grouped the Indian chief's lament with Buffy Sainte-Marie's "Now That The Buffalo's Gone" and classified them as "giving us a feeling of shame, a lack of pride in how we are treating other people." All classification systems were accepted and shared.

In applying strategies #2, #3, #4, you will be using the same procedure but applying it to beliefs, values and actions. Let me share some of the pupil responses in these areas with you.

In classifying on the basis of beliefs, most pupils viewed all the materials as expressing the belief that all people should have a land of their own. They viewed this belief as consonant with their own and used it as the criterion for grouping. Under beliefs, all materials were placed in one large group.

In applying strategy #3, classifying on the basis of values, in most cases, pupils placed the materials into two groups. The value they elicited was expressed in many ways: having a sense of belonging, being a people with a land, having pride in one's people and one's land. The pupils used this value as their criterion. The two groups which emerged were people who had achieved this sense of belonging to others and a land, and people who still sought to achieve this. Guthrie's song constituted one group and all the others made up the other group.

In applying strategy #4, classifying in terms of actions or behaviors, most pupils arrived at three groupings, urging people to help, giving up the cause and expressing one's feelings of sadness and pride. Pupils argued whether expressing one's feeling was a behavior and whether no action was a better category. Other pupils felt that when they took "no action" they were still behaving—they were choosing not to do something. Again as in the previous examples cited, interest, enthusiasm and involvement were great. Not only do pupils enjoy classifying in the affective domain, but they transfer this skill and apply it to their own life experiences.

Analyzing

An Operational Definition: When we are analyzing we are breaking down a problem, a concept, a pattern or a procedure into its component parts so that the sequence or hierarchy of the parts is made clear and the relationships and interrelationships are made explicit.

In the cognitive domain, we may analyze a short documentary film by listing the sequence of events, identifying those events which were major ones and those which were minor ones, tracing the relationship of one event to another, identifying the facts and the fallacies presented and attempting to see the whole in terms of its parts. Again in the cognitive domain, we may analyze a procedure such as how to use a microscope by breaking down this procedure into a step-by-step sequence.

Applying Analysis to the Affective Domain

In the affective domain, we are using analysis to break down a situation into its affective components—feelings, beliefs, attitudes, values and behaviors—and to determine the relationships between these components. Our purpose is to understand more fully the relationships between our feelings, beliefs, attitudes and values, and our behaviors. In addition, we are analyzing our values in order to identify our own hierarchy of values and thus better understand ourselves. In sum we are applying the process of analysis not to the general realm of knowledge but to "people" knowledge—to the knowledge of our actions, interactions and reactions with others in order to obtain greater insights into human behavior and our own functioning.

Structuring Questions for General Analysis

The following sample questions serve to promote analysis on the general or cognitive level:

- What are the key factors involved in this problem, situation of experiment?
- Describe the steps or procedures needed to _____.
- List the parts of X and describe how they are related.
- In solving X problem, list the sequential steps you would take.
- In reviewing a given situation, identify and list the relationships you have discovered.

Structuring Questions for Affective Analysis

The following are sample questions for applying analysis to the affective domain:

- Analyze the situation, story, etc., and identify any or all of the following: the feelings, the beliefs, the values and behaviors of the people involved.
- Analyze the situation, story, etc., and identify what you consider to be the key relationships between the feelings, beliefs, values and the behaviors of the people involved.
- Identify their values. What did they value most? Least? Not at all?

Strategies for Affective Analysis

The following three strategies may be used separately or may be combined into one strategy. The content and the specific group of pupils you are working with will determine your choice of strategies.

Strategy #1—Identifying Affective Components

Basic Structures:

- Given a personal experience, story, etc., describe what happened.
- How do you think X felt?
- Why do you think he felt this way?
- Did he have any firm beliefs? What were they?
- What did he do?
- Based on what he did, what do you think he valued?
- What would you have done in this situation if you were X?
- Based on what you would have done, what do you think you value?

Strategy #2—Identifying Values Hierarchies

Basic Structures:

- Given a personal experience, story, etc., describe what happened.
- What were some of the values of the people involved?
- Select one of these people. What were his values? Were there some things he valued more than others? What did he value the most? The least? Not at all?
- If you were in his place, what would you have valued most? Least? Not at all?

Strategy #3—Identifying Relationships

Basic Structures:

- Given a personal experience, story, etc., describe what happened.
- Describe how X felt.
- What do you think he believed?
- What did he do?
- What did he value?
- What relationships did you find between his feelings and his actions?
- What relationships did you find between his beliefs and his actions?
- What relationships did you find between his values and his actions?
- Image that you were X. Describe how you would have felt, what you would have believed, valued and done.
- Describe the relationships between your feelings, beliefs and values, and your actions.

Selecting Content for Affective Analysis

In applying the analysis strategies, you will find that role-play situations, stories, plays, films, narrative poems and television episodes are the best resources. The structured questions are invaluable when instructional time is limited. In selecting content there is no need to search for material which incorporates all of the affective components. As you use a variety of materials, pupils will have the opportunities to analyze feelings, beliefs, values and behaviors, relationships and value hierarchies. No one material has to meet all of these requirements. Teachers use these strategies flexibly, applying those structures which are most suited to the available content. In many cases, the curricular content serves as an opener for recalling personal experiences which then become the content for further analysis. In all cases, it is essential that the curricular content is directly related to the pupil. As you have already noted, the questions are always structured so that the pupil reacts to them on a personal basis. How do *you* feel about it; how would *you* have acted in this situation; what would *you* have valued? Affective analysis is just that—relating the analysis to the individual's concerns enabling the pupil to see how each of these components affect his own behavior.

Applying the Analysis Strategies to Curricular Content

Let's illustrate the use of some of the analysis strategies by applying them to curricular content. In the two illustrations which follow, the three strategies have been combined and are used flexibly in terms of the content.

Illustration #1

- Read the following lines:

    From break of day
    Till sunset glow
    I toil
    I dig my well,
    I dig my well,
    I plough my field,
    And earn my food
    And drink
    What care I
    Who rules the land
    If I
    Am left in peace?
- What is the writer saying?
- How do you think he feels?
- What reasons can be have for feeling this way?
- What does he believe?
- What does he value? What does he value most? Least? Not at all?
- What relationships exist between his feelings, his beliefs, his values and his day-to-day behaviors—his life?
- Put yourself in his place. You are this farmer. How would you feel? What would you believe? What would you value most? Least? Not at all?
- How would your feelings, beliefs, values affect your lifestyle and your day-to-day behavior?

Illustration #2

- Read the following paragraph:

    Let me be a free man— free to travel,
    free to stop, free to work, free to trade

where I choose, free to choose my own
teachers, free to follow the religion of
my fathers, free to think and talk
and act for myself—and I will
obey every law or submit to the
penalty.

- What is the writer saying?
- How do you think he feels?
- What reasons might he have for feeling this way?
- What does he believe?
- What does he value? What does he value most?
- How will his feelings, beliefs and values affect his daily behavior—his life?
- Put yourself in the writer's place. How do you feel about being free to do the things for which he is pleading?
- Do you believe that people should be free to do these things? Why or why not?
- How would your feelings, beliefs and values affect your daily life?

In Summary

If we as educators believe that our schools should provide pupils with opportunities to compare, classify and analyze their feelings, beliefs, values and behaviors, to understand how they are interrelated and how they influence and affect their day-to-day living, to examine their values and order them in terms of their own priorities and to look at themselves and determine whether they really value what they are doing and whether they are really doing what they value, then these process skills and those which follow are basic, invaluable tools. There is no need to say more!

5 Completing the Affective Cycle

Up to this point we have explored the affective domain by observing, associating, comparing, classifying and analyzing. The affective wheel has carried us almost to the completion of our journey. In this chapter we will reach the journey's end. We will be involved with the skills of interpreting and generalizing, divergent, critical and creative thinking. We will conclude with concept formation. Operational definitions, questioning techiniques, detailed strategies, and personal and curricular samples are all provided for direct classroom application.

Interpreting

An Operational Definition: When we are interpreting an experience or a body of data, we may be doing one or all of the following: we may be expressing the *meaning* the experience or data has for *us* or we may review the experience or data and then *construct inferences,* namely, explanations dealing with the causes(s) or conditions of the occurences; or we may study the experience or data and make *predictions* as to what might occur. Identifying the personal meaning of an experience or body of data, constructing inferences and making predictions are all forms of interpretation.

Let's begin with interpretation as an expression of meaning. We may start with an experience, a story, a poem or an art form. We review the experience, story or poem, etc., and describe what it means to *us.* In this case, we are highly subjective. We are putting meaning into the experience as well as taking meaning out. Our interpretations, in this case are neither right nor wrong; they simply are. What we are actually doing is *identifying the personal significance of the experience.*

Constructing Inferences

Let's continue with the process of interpretation as the construction of inferences. When we construct an inference, we are constructing an *explanation* of the occurrence; we are accounting for the occurrence. Something has happened; we were not there to observe it; we do not know how or why it occured other than it did. We make statements attempting to explain the how and or why of the happening. These statements are inferences. In some cases we are able to check our inferences; in others, the task is impossible.

Predicting

Prediction is another form of interpretation. In making predictions, just as we did in constructing inferences, we are moving beyond the experience or data. In this case we are describing what we anticipate could or might happen. Our predictions may range from those which we consider highly probable to probable, to possible, to improbable, and finally to impossible. Some predictions may be directly put to the test; others require the test of time.

It is evident at this point that in using all of the forms of interpretation we may move along a subjective-objective continuum. We may be subjective as we seek to derive personal meaning or highly objective when we attempt to check our inferences to assess their validity. Whether we operate at a subjective or objecitve level is determined by our specific purpose.

The Rationale For Interpretation

For all of us, interpretation in all of its forms, is an ongoing process. We use it constantly—when we read the newspapers, listen to music, watch television, attend an art exhibit, take trips and interact with each other.

In our daily encounters in the school setting, teachers and pupils are continuously interpreting each other's verbal and nonverbal behaviors. In terms of direct instruction, we have used this process extensively in the cognitive domain. Our pupils are required to interpret charts, graphs, to interpolate, to extrapolate, to conduct experiments, to construct inferences, hypotheses and make predictions. In the sciences, social science and mathematics, interpretation tends toward a high level of objectivity. It is only in the areas of language arts, literature and the fine arts that pupils are given the opportunities to use the various kinds of interpretation at the subjective level, but even in these areas expansion is needed.

All too often we have operated as if these processes were applicable only to the cognitive domain, losing sight of the fact that we do use them extensively on the affective level. As was stated previously, we are constantly abstracting personal meaning from all of our experiences and tossing aside those elements which lack this personal meaning, those which are irrelevant to us. The process of interpretation is precisely that—distinguishing between the relevant and irrelevant.

When we are dealing with interpretation as the construction of inferences, we may not always be aware of it, but we are applying this process to the affective domain. Based on what our family, friends and colleagues do, we infer how they feel, what they believe in and why they are doing what they are doing, and so determine how we are going to interact with them. Our operational world is permeated with inferences.

As in the case of inferring, we use predictions in dealing with the affective components of our lives. Based on what people do, believe and value, we make predictions as to what they are most likely to do in the future. Our predictions are by no means purely academic. In so many cases, we are compelled to rely on them to determine a personal course of action. Frequently we lose sight of how we as human beings use these processes *affectively*—how we apply these processes to diverse human beings and to the realm of imperfect "people knowledge." These, too, are facts of human behavior and, as our experiences have clearly shown us, processing these facts is the most difficult task of all. But these facts are crucial to our lives and therefore these process skills are equally crucial. Life is open to many interpretations; these skills are indispensable to us. What follows are questioning techniques and the strategies for the development of these interpretation skills.

Structuring Questions For General Interpretation

The following are questions for general use:

- Given an experience, story, song, poem, art form, place, etc., express what meaning it has for you.

- Given an experience, a body of data, etc., list the inferences you can draw from these.
- Given an experience, a description of an event, a film, etc., what predictions can you make?
- Given a chart, graph, detailed description, what predictions can you make that are highly probable, possible, least probable?
- Given the following data and a list of assumptions, compare the assumptions with the data and identify those assumptions which are warranted and those which are unwarranted.

Structuring Questions For Affective Interpretation

The following questions are applicable to the affective domain:

- Given a story, play, novel, poem, etc., prepare a written description of your interpretation of it.
- Study X photograph, describe what personal meaning it has for you.
- Read X cartoon, describe the personal message you receive.
- Study X cartoon and construct another cartoon which you feel should follow this one.
- Read only acts one and two of X play; write your own version of the third act, predicting what you think will happen.
- Listen to X ballad. Write a brief description explaining the possible reasons the songwriter had for writing this ballad.
- Read X editorial. List what you infer to be the motives, beliefs and values of the writer.
- Observe X film. Take the characters you identify with, place them in a new situation and predict what would happen.

Strategies For Affective Interpretation

The following three strategies are used for interpreting in the affective domain. We are dealing with interpretation as an expression of personal meaning, as the construction of inferences and as the formulation of predictions.

Strategy #1—Expressing Personal Meaning

Basic Structures:

- Given an event, story, poem, play, film, song, cartoon, photograph, illustration, film, article, essay, editorial, etc., express what meaning it has for you in terms of any of the following: your feelings, beliefs, values and actions.

Strategy #2—Constructing Inferences

Basic Structures:

- Given an event, story, poem, etc., review the material.
- Interpret the material and list the inferences you would make to explain: Why the people involved felt as they did, what their motivations were, why they believed as they did, what they valued, what they did and why they acted as they did.

Strategy #3—Making Predictions

Basic Structures:

- Given an event, story, poem, film, play, etc., read or view only the first parts as designated.
- Interpret what you have read or seen and list the predictions you would make in terms of what you think will happen, what you think each of the people involved will do and what the outcomes would be.
- Review your predictions and decide which of them you consider highly probable, probable or just possible.
- Complete your reading or viewing of the material and determine what actually occurred.
- Pretend you are a writer who has been asked to create a sequel to this story, play or film. Based on your knowledge of the characters, their beliefs, their values, construct a brief outline of your sequel, describing what you predict will happen.

Applying the Interpretation Strategies
To Curricular Content

Let's illustrate the application of these strategies to curricular content. The content available to use is extensive ranging from pictures, photographs and illustrations to novels and films.

Using Strategies #1, #2 and #3
With Primary Pupils

For primary pupils photographs, drawings and illustrations serve as excellent resources for initial interpretation. Mitsumasa Anno's book *Topsy-Turvies, Pictures To Stretch the Imagination*[1] is

1. Mitsumasa Anno, *Topsy-Truvies, Pictures to Stretch the Imagination.* New York: Weatherhill, Inc., 1970.

one such resource. Topsy-Turvies are exexactly what the title
denotes. They are strange, funny little men in very strange situations
doing strange things. The book has no words. It consists entirely of
pictures that do indeed stretch the imagination. The artist leaves all
the interpretations up to the viewer. Pupils interpret what they are
viewing, what personal meaning the pictures have for them (strategy
#1), what they think is happening in each picture and why they think
so (strategy #2), and predict what is going to happen (strategy #3). In
short, pupils go topsy-turvey in using all forms of interpretation.

Using Strategy #1—Expressing Personal Meaning—
With Elementary and Intermediate Pupils

- Read the following poem:

A Strange Place[2]

A strange place
A place unknown
Only a stone's throw
From the Human Race

It is not deep
It is not wide
It is not tall
Or small

This place you shall never find
For it is mine and mine alone.
Strangest of all
No place is so unknown.

Peter Rake

- Describe what personal meaning this poem has for you. What do
  you view as your strange place? How do you react to the lines
  "Strangest of all/No place is so unknown."
- Share your interpretations with your classmates.

Using Strategy #2—Constructing Inferences—
With Elementary and Intermediate Pupils

- Read the following poem:

I shook his hand
I touched him
How proud I felt.
He said "Hello" softly

2. Peter Rake, "A Strange Place" copyright © 1963 by the London Daily *Mirror*.

> I lost my voice,
> But in my mind I said
> everything

Ngaire Noffke[3]

- Describe what personal meaning this poem has for you.
- List some of the inferences you would make to explain: who could "he" be that made Ngaire so proud when he touched him? What kinds of feelings would Ngaire have experienced that caused him to lose his voice? What are some of the things Ngaire might have side in his mind?
- Share your inferences with your classmates.
- Can you recall any of your own experiences that are similar to Ngaire's? Share these with your classmates.

Using Strategy #3—Making Predictions— With Elementary and Intermediate Pupils

Stories, books, plays and films lend themselves readily to strategy #3—Making Predictions.

At the elementary level, a book such as Elizabeth Cooper's *The Fish From Japan*[4] is a fine choice. Pupils read about Harvey, who wants a pet and is very unhappy; even at school his classmate Karl will not allow him to feed the turtle. Harvey's uncle in Japan promises to send him a fish. Harvey is very excited, makes great preparations and tells his friends about it. But lo and behold, when the fish arrives, it is only a paper fish.

Pupils are asked to predict:

- What will happen?
- How do you think Harvey feels?
- How do you think his classmates will react?
- What will Karl say and do?
- Share your predictions with your classmates.
- Complete the story and check your predictions.

At the intermediate level, books are a major source for making predictions. For example, *The Greyhound*[5], by Helen Griffiths, is a good choice. The story centers around Jamie who needs money to buy food for his dog. He borrows the money from the leader of a gang. Consequently, he becomes involved with the gang and is forced

---

3. Ngaire Noffke, untitled poem in *Miracles,* ed. Richard Lewis, New York: Simon and Schuster, 1966.

4. Elizabeth K. Cooper, *The Fish from Japan,* New York: Harcourt Brace Jovanovich, Inc., 1969.

5. Helen Griffiths, *The Greyhound,* Garden City, N.Y.: Doubleday & Co., Inc., 1964.

to help in robberies. His relationship with his mother becomes tense and unbearable.

Pupils are asked to predict:

- How will Jamie handle the situation?
- What do you think Jamie values?
- Which values do you think Jamie will decide are most important to him?
- How do you think the story will end?
- Share your predictions with your classmates.
- Complete the book and check your predictions.

Using Strategy #1—Expressing Personal Meaning— With Secondary Pupils

At the secondary level there is no dearth of materials. In the sample given, we use a recording of *Song To A Seagull* by Joni Mitchell.

- Listen to *Song to a Seagull.*
- Express what meaning this song has for you.
- Select the lines that have a strong impact on you.
- Explaing why these lines have such personal meaning.
- Share your interpretations with your classmates.

Using Strategies #2, #3—Constructing Inferences and Making Predictions With Secondary Pupils

At this level books, novels, plays, etc., are numerous and readily applied. An example is Kristen Hunter's *The Soul Brothers and Sister Lou*[6]. The book centers on Lauretta who longs for a place to go after school, "someplace where she could talk, and have fun, and be with her friends." As a result of Lou's efforts a recreation center is created for teenagers in the black ghetto on Chicago's South Side. Lou's singing group comes to the attention of a recording studio and fame follows. Pupils are asked to make inferences and predictions in response to questions such as:

- Why do you suppose Lou became upset in the Soul Brothers and Sister Lou?
- How do you think Lauretta felt when she received the first check?
- Why do you think the city is providing money for the group?

6. Kristen Hunter. *The Soul Brothers and Sister Lou.* New York: Charles Scribner's Sons, 1968.

- What do you predict will happen next?
- How do you think the book will end?
- Share your predictions with your classmates.
- Complete the book and check your predictions.

The application of these questioning techniques, strategies, and the activities they suggest demonstrates that the process of interpretation provides diverse, stimulating and creative possibilities for meaningful learning.

Generalizing

An Operational Definition: When we are generalizing we are observing specific situations or phenomena, comparing them, noting their similarities and formulating a rule or principle which is applicaable to all of them.

The Rationale For Cognitive and Affective Generalization

Whether we are consciously aware of it or not, we live on the basis of our generalizations, we pattern our behaviors on generalizations. Specifics and details are readily forgotten but generalizations are retained. Learning in the cognitive domain becomes a more efficient and effective process simply because specifics and details have been ordered, organized and subsumed under rules and principles.

In the affective domain, generalizations control and determine our behaviors and goals—in essence, our lifestyle. Our beliefs, attitudes and values are all rules, principles and generalizations. If we accept the generalization that wealthy people are happy people, we may drive ourselves to acquire this wealth; if we believe intelligent people are well-read people, we may read extensively, if we believe that travel broadens the mind, we may travel; if we believe that sociable people drink X cola, we may drink X cola. If we view the generalization as valid and relevant to ourselves, we are most likely to operate on that basis.

We have only to view the T.V. commercials and magazine advertisements to discover how values generalizations have been used to convince us that X,Y or Z product will drastically change our lives.

Many worthless and totally useless products are hooked onto generalized values. The assumption is simply that if we identify with these values, we will buy the product; if we identify with the people who possess the characteristics we prize—the "beautiful" people, the "cultured" people, the "successful" people—we will buy the product they endorse.

We live by the rules of the game. Too often these rules, generalizations and principles lack validity. Too often our beliefs, attitudes and values in terms of human behavior are based on false assumptions. If our youth are to cope with realities and become autonomous individuals, they must develop not only the skills of generalizing but of testing these generalizations, of assessing their beliefs, and of validating and reconstructing their value systems based on the changing times.

As educators we have just barely begun to touch upon the significant area of human behavior in terms of its basic generalizations. This area has in the past been postponed and categorized as "courses" in psychology, anthropology and sociology, as if our pupils had no practical use for these disciplines until they became seniors in high school or were fortunate enough to go to college. Realistically, our pupils have had *minimal* exposure to such questions as: what are the key factors which motivate people to act and to strive? What kinds of diverse beliefs are prevalent in our society, and in other societies? What kinds of attitudes and diverse values exist in this multi-society, in this pluralistic society? It would appear that since life begins at birth and not at the point where pupils complete their high school education that the content of people knowledge is relevant from primary school and onward.

Interweaving Affect With Cognition

In the past decade prominent psychologists, social scientists and educators have urged that more of the social sciences be incorporated into school texts. A variety of courses of study have emerged fostered by grants but unfortunately the trend has not caught on. Other educators have attempted a more direct approach such as focusing directly on values clarification. These materials are excellent, but as has been the case in so many educational endeavors, they must be integrated into the existing disciplines. Our curriculum in most schools is a patchwork of disciplines. The major threads of affect and cognition have not been adequately interwoven into this patchwork quilt. Many new social studies texts are now attempting to achieve this. But, as previously, this interweaving of affect and cognition into one discipline is not the solution. The interweaving must take place into all disciplines. As classroom teachers and school administrators we can achieve this; the "weaving" is up to us. The most significant generalizations—those dealing with beliefs, values and human behavior, regardless of the labels we have assigned to them—must be incorporated into the total school curriculum, starting at the elementary level. If formal schooling is to educate youngsters to understand the "world," it would seem logical that they start by just understanding themselves—understanding the generalizations by which they direct their own lives; the drives, needs, beliefs, attitudes and values which determine their own behaviors, and the diversity of drives, needs, beliefs, attitude and values which result in differing life styles, conflicts of interests and significant human problems requiring cooperative solutions.

Generalizing, identifying generalizations, determining their validity in situational contexts and applying generalizations to life situations are vital life skills. In the past and, unfortunately, in the present, generalizing in the affective domain has been limited. The generalizations which we were taught and in the majority of cases as they are taught now are induced in a highly didactic mode; their affective implications and application are presented on an intellectual level rather than experienced at the gut level. These gut level experiences and expressions are what restore relevancy to the school curriculum. This restoration is our task. What follows are questioning techniques and strategies for beginning this restoration.

Structuring Questions For Generalizing

In constructing generalizing questions for either domain the basic structures are the following:

- Given the following data, charts, graphs, objects, etc., *what big statement can you make that is applicable to all?*
- Given the following words, sentences, mathematics operations, etc., *what rule can you formulate?*
- Given the following geometric forms, plant specimens, rock samples, etc., *what characteristics are common to all?*

Affective Questions For Generalizing

- Given a variety of sample situations, etc., within the limits of this data, what generalizations can you make (all people, most people, some people) on how needs affect behavior?
- Given a variety of sample situations, etc., within the confines of the data, what generalization or proportional generalization can you make on how motivation or goals affect behavior?
- Given a variety of sample situations, etc., within the confines of the data, what generalizations or proportional generalizations can you

make on how feelings affect behavior or how behavior may indicate the feelings one is experiencing?

- Given a variety of sample situations, etc., within the confines of the data, what generalization can you make on how beliefs and values affect behavior?
- Given a variety of sample situations, etc., within the confines of the data, what generalization can you make on how people respond to conflicting values?

Strategies For Generalizing In The Affective Domain
Strategy #1—Generalizing In Terms of Motivations and Behaviors

Basic Structures:

Given a variety of sample situations from stories, plays, novels, films, etc., analyze these by responding to the following questions:

- In each sample, what were the people's motivations? What did they want to achieve?
- Compare their motivations. How were they similar? Different?
- How did they go about achieving their goals?
- Were there commonalities in their methods of attaining their goals?
- Within the limits of the data you are given, can you make a generalization or generalizations (all people, most people, some people who seek to _____ will _____) on how motivation affects behavior?
- Can you recall other experiences, personal experiences, ones you have witnessed or read about that support your generalization or refute it?
- Share your generalization with your classmates.

Strategy #2—Generalizing In Terms of Feelings and Behaviors

Basic Structures:

- Given a variety of sample situations from stories, plays, novels, films, etc., analyze these by responding to the following questions:
- In each sample, how did the people react to the situation? What feelings did they express or demonstrate?
- Compare their feelings. How were they similar, different?
- In each sample, how did the people respond to their feelings; how did they handle them; what did they do?

- Compare their behaviors in response to their feelings. Were they similar in any way; were they different?
- Within the limits of the samples you have, can you make any kind of generalization (all people, most people, some people who believe that _____ will _____) on how people's beliefs affect their behavior?
- Can you recall other experiences, personal experiences, ones you have witnessed, heard about or read that support or refute your generalization?
- Share your generalization with your classmates.

Strategy #3—Generalizing In Terms of Beliefs and Behaviors

Basic Structures:

Given a variety of sample situations from stories, plays, novels, films, etc., analyze these by responding to the following questions:

- In each sample, what were the people's beliefs?
- Compare their beliefs. How were they similar? Different?
- In each sample, how did the people demonstrate their beliefs in terms of their actions?
- Compare their behaviors. Were there any similarities; differences?
- Within the limits of the samples you have, can you make any kind of generalization (all people, most people, some people who value _____ will _____) on how people's values affect their behavior?
- Can you recall other experiences, personal experiences, ones you have seen, heard about or read about that support or refute your generalization?
- Share your generalization with your classmates.

Strategy #4—Generalizing In Terms of Values and Behaviors

Basic Structures:

Given a variety of sample situations from stories, plays, novels, films, etc., analyze these by responding to the following questions:

- In each sample, identify the individual's problem.
- Analyze his behavior in response to his problem and identify what he valued.

- Was there a conflict of values? If so, which value was most important to him?
- Did he have to compromise in any way?
- Compare how each of these people responded to their values. Were their behaviors similar or different? In what ways were they similar? Different?
- Within the limits of the samples you have, can you make any kind of generalization (all people, most people, some people who value _____ will _____) on how people's values affect their behavior?
- Can you recall other experiences, personal experiences, ones you have witnessed, heard about or head about that support or refute your generalization?
- Share your generalization with your classmates.

Applying the Strategies of Generalizing To Curricular Content

Let's illustrate how we would apply a few of these strategies in the classroom. Pupils are presented with the following account:

Joining the Tornados

A new electronics plant has opened in town and many new families have moved in. Tony, Paul, Marc and Ken are newcomers; this is their third week at Morris Middle School. They have all decided to join a boy's club called the Tornados. As Tony says, "Regular guys need friends." Tony's parents are very upset. They don't want Tony joining any "gang." Paul, Marc and Ken are in the same situation. They say their parents have forbidden them to associate with the Tornados.

Paul says he is joining the group and that's that. "My parents choose their friends and I'll choose mine. I told them I was going to join." Marc has decided to wait for a while and to discuss the situation further after his parents have cooled off. "I'm going to try to make them see it my way." Ken has decided to join but it's to be a secret. No one is to tell his parents that he's a member. Tony is very upset and tells the group, "I respect my folks. I want to join but it will really hurt them. I can't lie to them. It just would not feel right so I'll have to forget it."

In applying strategy #1, in which the pupils are asked to generalize in terms of motivations and behaviors, the pupils identify the goal or motivation as wanting to belong to a group and have friends. In comparing the motivation of each of the boys, they decide the motivation is the same in all cases. In their attempts to achieve their goal, the pupils find that the boys differ in their methods. The generalizations which evolve are: Most people want to belong to a group and have friends, and will seek to do so. Although most people are motivated to belong to a group and have friends, their methods of achieving this will differ.

In applying strategy #2, in which the pupils are asked to generalize in terms of feelings and behaviors, the pupils described Tony as having strong feelings of disappointment, sadness, frustration and anger as well as caring very much about hurting his parents. They felt that Paul and Ken felt disappointment, frustration and anger, but did not show great concern about their parents' feelings. They described Ken as having similar feelings, but that he also cared deeply about his parents' feelings and would try to talk with them. The pupils thought all of the boys had mixed feelings and that their behaviors were certainly different. The generalizations which evolved were that: Most people may experience the same feelings but will behave differently in response to these feelings; people's feelings affect their behavior.

Strategy #3, Generalizing in Terms of Beliefs and Behavior, was not applicable to this sample and was not used.

In applying strategy #4, in which pupils were asked to generalize in terms of values and behaviors, the pupils identified the values as friendship, family and honesty. They saw that all the boys strongly valued friendship and belonging to a group, that Tony and Marc strongly valued their parents, that both Tony and Marc valued honesty and that Ken did not. All agreed that there was a definite conflict of values in valuing friends, parents and honest relationships. The generalizations which evolved were: Most people may hold the same or similar values but will behave in many different ways in expressing these values; people's behaviors usually reflect their values; most people expreience conflicting values in solving problems and their solutions will differ based on the strength of these values.

In sum, pupils and teachers find these generalizing experiences not only exciting and interesting but tend to use them extensively. Their relevancy results in their continuous use.

Divergent Thinking

An Operational Definition: When we are using divergent thinking, we are exploring a problem or situation and attempting to discover a variety of options, choices and alternatives which are open to us. We allow our thoughts to diverge, to move freely from the usual to the unusual. Our purpose is to find a diversity of alternatives.

Too often our learned experiences restrict us. We are accustomed to doing things in prescribed ways. We have become functionally fixated—we see things in their usual context. Pencils and paper are for writing, but I am certain that if we sat down together and brainstormed we could probably come up with a list of at least one hundred other uses for pencils and paper. Many of us have been trained to see things in terms of their usual functions and their common uses; our task is to remove the assigned functions and the specific context and to explore freely.

To date, divergent thinking has been used extensively in the cognitive domain. Many of us will recall the year when divergent thinking was "discovered" and became the major tool in classes of creative writing. Since then it has been applied to art, music, social studies and the sciences. Its use was a major breakthrough, for pupils soon realized that there was not necessarily only one solution to a given problem, that there was not always one correct answer, that there was not always one prescribed procedure which had to be utilized, but that there were many. In that real world out there, there are many options and alternatives yet to be discovered and tested!

Applying Divergent Thinking To the Affective Domain

One option which was available to us as educators and which had been overlooked was the applicability of divergent thinking to the affective domain. In our daily experiences, alternatives, options and choices are always available to us. They are almost never closed; we just believe they are! Our most significant experiences—those of greatest personal relevance—are by no means purely cognitive, but are heavily loaded with affective components. It is in this area where divergent thinking can be most productive. There are many ways in which we may react to a given situation, there are many ways in which we can cope with our problems, there are many possible decisions we may reach. In the processes of resolving conflicts of feelings, emotions, beliefs and value systems, divergent thinking is critical. Therefore, it was not only logical but definitely practical to use this tool. Life offers us many paths, we must be aware of them in order to explore them.

Structuring Questions For The
General Use of Divergent Thinking

- How many different ways are there to solve problem X?
- How many different problems could arise from situation X?
- How many different patterns can you create with X materials?
- How many different ways can you classify these objects, words, ideas, etc.?
- How many different conclusions can you draw from this data?
- How many different sources or error can account for the results of your experiment?
- How many different uses can you find for object Y?
- List at least two alternative responses to the following questiions:
  - a. What would have happened if John F. Kennedy had not been assassinated?
  - b. What would have happened if the Nixon tapes had not existed?
  - c. What would have happened if the Viet Nam War had continued?

Structuring Questions for the
Affective Use of Divergent Thinking

- In this situation, how many other ways could X have reacted to the problem?
- In solving the problem, how many other alternatives were available to Y?
- What are some of the things X could have done to change the situation?
- How many different views can we anticipate in terms of this issue?
- How many different means can we use to involve and interest people in this issue?
- What are the various consequences if the issue is resolved in one way? In the other way?
- List at least three responses to the following questions:
  - a. List at least three things you would do if you suddenly received a large sum of money.

b. List at least three things you would do if you were free to do anything you wanted to do.

c. List at least three changes you would make if you had the resources to create your own society.

Strategies For Divergent Thinking In the Affective Domain

The following two strategies are used for promoting divergent thinking in the affective domain. Strategy #1 deals with situations and strategy #2 deals with issues.

Strategy #1—Dealing With Situations

Basic Structures:

- Given a personal experience, event, story, etc., describe what occurred.
- How did the individuals involved feel about it?
- In what other ways could they have reacted to this situation?
- Why did they feel as they did?
- What did they do?
- What alternatives did they think they had?
- What other alternative actions were available to them?
- What possible reasons could they have had for selecting their course of action?
- Why do you think they chose that particular course of action?
- What were the consequences?
- What other consequences could have been?
- How did they feel about the consequences?
- What other reactions could they have had to these consequences?

Strategy #2—Dealing With Issues

Basic Structures:

- Given key issues such as drug control, gun control, mercy killing, school integration, welfare programs, etc., describe the issue.
- Identify all of the possible positions one can take on this issue.
- List all of the different arguments that might be offered.
- Based on each position, identify all of the possible affective reactions one might anticipate.
- Taking each position, identify all of the possible consequences.

Applying Affective Divergent Thinking Strategies To Curricular Content

Strategy #1—Dealing With Situations

- Pupils are given a situation such as the following:

School is almost over. The summer is approaching. Bill is trying to make plans. He has decided that his life's goal is to become an artist. He feels he has the talent and wants to spend the summer painting. He believes that if you really work hard at something you will succeed, but that you have to devote all of your time and effort if you are going to make it happen. Bill's family is poor. They could use the extra money Bill would make if he takes a job in the factory for the summer. Bill knows that the factory work is dull and boring. He doesn't know what to do. When he thinks of spending the summer painting, he feels excited, but he also feels guilty. He should help his folks. When he thinks of spending the summer working in the factory, he also feels guilty. He should develop his talent. Bill is trying to explore all of the alternatives open to him.

- Pupils are asked to respond to the following questions:
- How would you describe Bill's problem?
- How does Bill feel about his situation?
- Why does he feel as he does?
- What is his conflict?
- What alternatives does Bill think he has?
- What other alternatives do you think are available to him?
- Examine the alternatives you have suggested and describe at least two consequences of each.

Strategy #2—Dealing With Issues

- Pupils are presented with an issue such as the following:

Should television stations be permitted to continue to show movies and serials which contain acts of violence? Are these programs teaching us to become more violent? Are they causing us to become so accustomed to violence that we are numb to it, that we accept it as normal? Or are these programs depicting reality: are they telling us that people are violent or can be violent, and that we must learn to deal with it?

- Pupils are asked to respond to the following questions:
- Identify all the possible positions one can take on this issue.

- List all the different arguments that might be offered.
- Based on each position, describe the kinds of feelings you think people would express.
- Taking each position, identify what you view as some of the possible consequences.

Having become well-acquainted with the questions and strategies of divergent thinking, we can appreciate its salience in exploring alternatives and in identifying the "multiple choices" of life. "So many things are possible just as long as you don't know they're impossible."[7]

As we deal with the process of critical thinking or decision making which follows, the fundamental value of divergent thinking as a condition and prerequisite for this process will become distinctly evident.

Critical Thinking

An Operational Definition: When we are using critical thinking, we are involved with a series of process skills for the specific purpose of making a decision. We may start with a problem situation or an issue. Sequentially, we acquire factual data and "feeling" data; we analyze the data, distinguishing between the relevant and the irrelevant; we explore relationships, options and alternatives, and evaluate the data not only on a factual level but in terms of our feelings, beliefs and values, and then make a decision on the basis of this evaluation.

The Affective Components of Critical Thinking

From the above definition, it is obvious that critical thinking is not the mere application of cold logic to a problem or issue, but entails far more. The decisions we make and live with must be right, good and effective for us. Personally good, right and effective translated in operational terms means that our decisions are not only based on factual data but that our decisions reflect personal data— our feelings, beliefs, attitudes and values. Any personal decision— what we are planning to commit ourselves to—must be something we highly value, something we whole-heartedly believe in and are willing to risk doing, feeling it is right for us. Our criteria are both facts and "feelings."

When we are delegated the responsibility for making decisions pertinent to others, these affective criteria are equally important. How many times have we made decisions that were extremely

7. Norton Juster, *The Phantom Tollbooth,* New York: Random House, 1961.

rational and that were in keeping with the factual data, only to discover that this decision was totally inoperative? On the cognitive level—on paper—it was a great decision, bound to work to solve the problem; with people, it was devastating. We had failed to take into account the feelings, attitudes and values of the individuals involved. To view decision making or critical thinking as applicable only to the cognitive domain is analogous to viewing the world as totally automatized, devoid of free-spirited, self-directed human beings. The most productive decisions are those based on the analysis and evaluation of both cognitive and affective components.

The Rationale For Critical Thinking

As educators we would be the first to acknowledge that critical thinking is an indispensable skill. At times life seems to be just one decision after another. Each day we find that the number of decisions confronting us is increasing at a phenomenal rate. Yet in our schools, we provide our pupils with a relatively few opportunities to become responsible decision makers. Decisions are made for our pupils rather than by our pupils. How can our pupils learn to decide if we make their decisions for them? Decision making is certainly not relegated only to adults. Our pupils are faced with hundreds of choices throughout their years of formal schooling. What should I be? Who should I choose as my friends? Should I give up some of my friends because my parents don't like them? Should I go out for sports? Should I learn to play a musical instrument? Should I try drugs? Should I work for an A? Which courses should I take? Should I go to college? Which college should I choose? Decisions, decisions and more decisions. Decisions which mold their lives; critical decisions which they must learn to make and which we must teach them *how* to make.

We have only to review some of the findings of research such as Donald Super and Phoebe Overstreet, *The Vocational Maturity of Ninth-Grade Boys,*[8] John Flanagan's *Project Talent*[9] to recognize the dire need for helping pupils learn how to make decisions. Flanagan's and Super and Overstreet's findings concur that generally junior and senior high school students are poor decision makers and experience difficulty in making curricular choices in high school, in choosing occupations and in selecting appropriate colleges.

Instruction in critical thinking need not be postponed until

8. Donald Super and Phoebe L. Overstreet, *The Vocational Maturity of Ninth-Grade Boys,* New York: Columbia University Press.

9. John Flanagan, "Project Talent" in the *American High School Student,* University of Pittsburgh, 1964.

pupils reach junior or senior high school. Pupils at all levels should be provided with opportunities to develop these decision-making skills, to practice these skills by applying them to classroom and out-of-classroom situations. Up to this point, we have focused on the process skills which enable pupils to explore and clarify their feelings, beliefs, values and behaviors, to identify the variety of alternatives available to them in dealing with problem-solving situations. The skills of critical thinking follow naturally since critical thinking is based on a knowledge of one's self and one's values. One cannot make choices, set goals for one's self and plan ahead without this self-knowledge.

If we firmly believe in the development of autonomous individuals who are able to cope realistically with change, then the need for critical thinking is evident. The questioning techniques and strategies which follow are the tools with which we may achieve this goal.

Structuring Questions For the
General Use of Critical Thinking

- Given X problem and two or more alternative solutions, which one would you select? Why?
- Given X issue and three viewpoints, which viewpoint would you favor? Why?
- Given two or more alternates or choices, which would you select? Why?

Structuring Questions Focusing On the
Affective Components of Critical Thinking

- Explore the alternative solutions to X problem and describe your feelings in regard to each.
- Explore the alternative solutions to X problem and describe your beliefs in regard to each.
- Assess the alternative solutions to X problem and identify the values each one reflects.
- Evaluate the alternative solutions to problem X and identify the conflicting values.
- List the values reflected in the alternative solutions and rank them in order of their importance to you.
- Evaluate each of the solutions offered and list the risks involved in each.

- Identify the solution to problem X which offers you the least risks.
- Identify the solution to problem X which offers you the most risks.
- Identify the solution to problem X which offers you the greatest number of advantages.

Strategies For Critical Thinking
In the Affective Domain

The following two strategies are used for promoting critical thinking and incorporate the affective as well as cognitive components. The strategies are similar in format. Strategy #1 deals with problem situations and strategy #2 deals with current issues.

Strategy #1—Dealing With Problem Situations

Given a problem and alternative courses of action:

- Identify the facts.
- Review the alternative courses of action. Can you think of or create any others?
- What are the pros and cons of each alternative in terms of the facts?
- Examine the beliefs involved. Which course of action is most consistent with your strongest beliefs?
- Assess the alternative solutions and identify the values each reflects.
- List the values and rank them in order of their importance to you.
- Which values are in conflict with each other?
- Which course of action is most consistent with your highest values?
- Evaluate each of the alternative solutions and list the risks involved.
- Which course of action offers you the least risks? The most risks?
- Which course of action offers you the greatest number of advantages?
- Which course of action is:
  (a) most consistent with your strongest beliefs
  (b) most consistent with your highest values
  (c) most acceptable in terms of the risks involved
  (d) most advantageous to you
- Select the best solution for you and list the reasons for your choice.

Strategy #2—Dealing With Issues

Given an issue with two or more viewpoints:

- Identify the facts.
- Review the viewpoints offered. Are there others you can add?
- List the pros and cons of each viewpoint in terms of the facts.
- Evaluate each viewpoint in terms of the advantages it has for you, for others, and for most people.
- Assess each viewpoint and identify the values it reflects.
- Which viewpoint is most consistent with your beliefs and values?
- Evaluate each viewpoint in terms of the advantages it has for you, for others, and for most people
- Assess each viewpoint in terms of the risks involved for you and for others.
- Select the viewpoint or stand you will take based on your beliefs, values, the advantages, and the risks involved. List the reasons for your choice.

Applying the Critical Thinking Strategies To Personal and Curricular Content

Strategy #1—Dealing With Problem Situations

Let's apply this critical thinking strategy to the case of Bill, the young man who was faced with the problem of deciding whether he would spend his summer developing his talents as an artist or working in a factory to assist his folks financially.

In discussing the options available to Bill, the pupils came up with the following: (1) Bill could compromise. He could spend one month of his vacation working in the factory and thereby help his folks, and one month at his painting. (2) Another form of compromise suggested was that Bill work part-time at the factory, possibly mornings, and paint during the afternoons. (3) Bill should devote the entire summer to his art and keep in mind that in the long run his efforts will be rewarded. (4) Bill should work full-time at the factory and paint in the evenings. His first obligation should be to his parents.

Given Bill's problem and the alternatives offered, the pupils proceed to:

- Identify the facts in Bill's case.
- Review the alternative courses of action available to him.

- List the pros and cons of each alternative based on the facts.
- List Bill's beliefs in terms of his obligations to his parents, work and success.
- List Bill's values. Identify the conflicting values in Bill's case.
- Evaluate the alternatives and list the risks involved.
- Evaluate the alternatives and review the advantages of each.
- Determine which course of action is
  (a) most consistent with Bill's beliefs
  (b) most consistent with Bill's values
  (c) provides Bill with the most satisfaction and least guilt
  (d) most acceptable in terms of the risks Bill must take
  (e) most advantageous to all concerned.
- Select the best solution for Bill and briefly summarize reasons for their choice.

Strategy #2—Dealing With Issues

Let's apply this strategy to the issue we used with divergent thinking.

Should television stations be permitted to continue to show programs which contain acts of violence?

- Given the issue, pupils proceed to identify the facts. In this case, pupils researched the issue and found the data inconclusive. There were no hard facts to substantiate that viewing violence on television promoted violent behavior in children or adults.
- Pupils offered viewpoints on the issue, the position given were (1) Yes, television stations should continue showing these programs. (2) No, they should not be allowed to continue this practice. (3) Yes, they should—but only during adult viewing hours.
- Pupils listed the pros and cons of each viewpoint based on the studies they had read.
- Pupils listed their beliefs such as: I believe viewing violence promotes violence in young and old alike; I believe viewing violence has no effect on behavior if people value and respect each other; I believe that viewing violence must serve to meet some needs but doesn't have to result in violent behavior.
- Pupils listed the values they felt each viewpoint reflected. Values such as respect for human life, money, success, law and order were given.
- Pupils listed the advantages of each viewpoint emphasizing that the paucity of information limited them.

- Pupils listed the risks involved in terms of each viewpoint. Those who opposed the practice felt we were risking increased violence, creating a numbness to violence and promoting an acceptance of violence as a normal reaction to situations. Those who viewed the practice as harmless felt there were no risks involved.

- Pupils then proceeded to take a stand based on their evaluation of the available data, their beliefs and values, and the risks involved, and then summarized their reasons for their stand.

In sum, recognizing the critical value of decision making in school and life situations, we as educators should provide our pupils with these significant opportunities. These are life skills. No more can be said and much more can be done. The decision is ours.

Creative Thinking

An Operational Definition: When we are thinking creatively, we are using feelings, emotions, concepts, ideas, words and objects, developing them, organizing them reorganizing them and arriving at a product or solution which is novel, original, unexpected and imaginative in its new form.

The Rationale for Creative Thinking

Traditionally creative thinking has been applied to the cognitive domain in our language arts and fine arts classrooms. Although it is quite obvious to us that a major facet of creativity comes from the affective domain, from our feelings, our emotive reactions to living, we have ignored the obvious and minimized it. We have not allowed the affective blood to flow freely and mix with its cognitive component. We have stifled its flow. It is not at all surprising that creativity flows at the elementary level of education but merely "drips" at the secondary level. The pupil has been greatly "intellectualized" by the time he reaches secondary school. He has learned to control his feelings and emotions: he has learned to submerge and repress them. Rather than stimulating affective awareness and integrating it with cognitive growth, we have compartmentalized it. To constrict and restrict creativity to specific areas of learning is to inhibit its growth; this is not our goal. We need creative people who are sensitive to all aspects of life, who are able to freewheel, to roam mentally and affectively, to go beyond the commonplace, to invent, to be original, to be fluent and flexible with feelings as well as ideas, to delve and explore, to sit "on the shelf" or in some quiet place and imagine, dream, fantasize, "to look at the familiar and make it strange," and "look at the strange and make it familiar."

The concept of creative thinking is not a new one. We are familiar with the works of Getzels, Jackson, Guilford, Lowenfeld, Parnes, Torrance, Osborn and Gordon. Brainstorming, synectics and guided fantasy are tools at our disposal. We have but to use them. Therefore, when applied to the affective domain, creative thinking becomes an invaluable tool. It serves as a vital means for self-exploration, self-expression and obtaining increased "knowledge" of one's self. In addition it serves as an integrative tool enabling us to relate external reality—the world of events, substantive knowledge and intellectual activity with the internal world of feelings, emotions, drives and values.

Structuring Questions For Creative Thinking

Questions such as the following are for general use and have been applied to the cognitive domain:

- Make up a story _____.
- Create or design a _____.
- Imagine that _____; what would happen?
- Change the beginning, middle or end of a story.
- Change the lyrics of _____ song.
- Devise a system or procedure for _____.
- Invent a language, a number system, a tool, etc. _____.
- Compose a song.
- Construct a collage.

Strategies For Creative Thinking
In the Affective Domain

These one-step strategies deal with the individual's self-concept, his relationships with significant others, his beliefs, values and visions of the future.

Creative Strategies For Developing Self-Concept

- Create a story, a poem, a song or a play about yourself.
- Draw a self-portrait.
- Pretend you are an "object" for sale.
- Write an advertisement so that someone would "buy" you.
- Create something that expresses the real you.
- Write an essay about yourself using the first person.

- Write an essay about yourself using the third person.
- Create a story, a poem or a song about the ideal you.
- Express a dream you had. Use words, music, art or any media you wish.
- Create a fantasy about yourself when you realize a dream or a hope.
- Identify with another form of life, plant or animal. Describe being that organism.
- Identify with an object. Describe being that object.

Creative Strategies Dealing With Relationships With Significant Others

- Think of one of your best friends. Write a description of yourself as he would see you.
- Pretend you are one of your parents or brothers or sisters; create a story, poem or song describing how they see you.
- Fantasize about someone in your family. Create a story, a poem or a song about one of them.
- Think about one of your favorite teachers. Call him or her Mr. or Mrs. X. Write a description of yourself as he or she would see you.
- Imagine what you would consider an ideal friend. Write a story or poem or compose a song about him or her.
- Someone has given you a beautiful island where you may spend your summer vacations. You are permitted to bring five other people with you. Write about the five people you would invite to share your island. They can be real or imaginary.

Creative Strategies Dealing With Feelings, Beliefs, Values and Visions of the Future

- Express happiness or joy by writing a poem, story, song or painting a picture.
- Draw a picture of anger.
- Express sadness using prose, poetry, music, painting or sculpture.
- Select a belief, one you feel strongly about and express that belief in any form you wish—words, music, art, photography, etc.
- Select a value by which you live. Express this value using any medium you wish.

- Select a person you value greatly. Write a poem, story or song about this person.

- Select an object you value greatly. Express your feelings about this object using any medium of your choice.

- Identify an issue which is of vital concern to you. Pretend that you are able to move through time and discuss this issue with any famous person in the past whom you admire and respect. Conduct the dialogue and record it.

- Pretend you had but one week to live; describe what you would do.

- Imagine that someone offers to give you one thing in the world which you prize above all things. What would you choose? Express your choice in any way you wish.

- Imagine that you were given the power to make your town or city the most beautiful one in the world. Describe what it would be like. Use any medium or combination of media you wish.

- Fantasize about a utopian society in which you would live. Express your fantasy in words, music or any art form.

Applying the Creative Strategies To Personal and Curricular Content

The one-step strategies which have been provided are self-illustrative and are directly applicable to the classroom. The content in each case has been personal content, providing opportunities for the pupil to creatively express his feelings, beliefs, values and hopes based on his experiential background as well as his fantasy life.

Making the transition to curricular content is readily done, as evidenced by the following samples.

In language arts, pupils read a poem such as "Dreams."

Dreams[10]

Hold fast to dreams
For if dreams die
Life is a broken-winged bird
That cannot fly.

Hold fast to dreams
For when dreams go
Life is a barren field
Frozen with snow.

Langston Hughes

10. Langston Hughes, "Dreams" in *The Dream Keeper and Other Poems*, New York: Alfred Knopf, Inc., 1967.

Pupils are asked to create a story or poem or painting or song about dreams that were realized or dreams that were frozen.

In social studies, pupils may have been studying different cultures, focusing on the political, economic and social forces operating in these cultures. Pupils may be asked to assume the role of a newspaper reporter and write a story about the people, their lifestyles, beliefs and values, and the major problems confronting them. Or pupils may assume the role of being a member of that culture and create a poem, song, story or diary depicting their life in that society.

In science, pupils may have been studying ecology and focusing on the crucial problems of pollution, energy conservation and population growth. Pupils may be asked to create slogans, editorials, posters, plays and songs to stimulate constructive action on the part of the public.

In mathematics pupils may have been exposed to the workings of a computer and the vast impact of computer technology on our society. Pupils may be asked to create any variety of products they choose to depict the advantages or disadvantages of computers in their lives.

In art and music, having been exposed to a variety of forms, pupils may be encouraged to express their reactions to these forms and to create their own products depicting the effects of these forms on their personal lives.

In the area of health, pupils may have obtained extensive knowledge on drug abuse, alcoholism and smoking—issues with which they will have to deal. Stories, poems, tapes, video tapes, filmstrips, slide shows, posters, photographs and diagrams are products pupils may create to express their feelings, beliefs, attitudes and values.

In sum, identifying curricular content for creativity presents no problem. In all content areas, if we present these materials so that pupils interact with them on a personal basis, seeing how these knowledges affect their lives and their future, relevancy will be achieved and creative expression will flow. The development of creative individuals is our goal and we certainly have the means to achieve it!

Concept Formation—Defining a Concept

Before we define concept formation in operational terms, it is essential that we are in agreement as to what constitutes a concept.

The diverse concepts of concepts which are currently found in our texts are indeed misleading. Principles, rules and generalizations have been mislabeled concepts. They are not concepts; they are integral parts of concepts. A concept is a broad understanding—an enlarged mental image. Let's exemplify this. Everything you and I know about love constitutes our concept of love. As we encounter or experience loving situations, loving people, loving pets, loving literature— "lovingness" in different contexts—we abstract the essence of love, our concept of love emerges, changes and grows. Based on our own experiential background, we build a conceptual framework of love in which we can now store additional experiences. Principles, generalizations and rules pertaining to love will become part of the framework, but they are not the framework per se.

We order our lives in terms of our concepts or conceptual framework. If events occur which do not fit into an available framework, we construct one. The concepts we deal with vary; they may be concrete or abstract. A concrete concept is an understanding that can be directly perceived by the senses: the concepts of horse, orange, train, for example. An abstract concept is an understanding or mental image of an intangible that is represented by some symbol; for example, the concept of triangle, circle, one hundred, under, over, love, joy, happiness, anger, fear, etc.

Now equipped with a concept of a concept and illustrations of both concrete and abstract concepts, let's return to the process of conceptualizing—how is it done?

Conceptualizing

An Operational Definition: When we are forming concepts or conceptualizing, we are observing or experiencing aspects of the concept, describing these aspects, qualities or characteristics, comparing them and then abstracting or "drawing out" those qualities and synthesizing them into the concept. We are then able to generalize and apply this concept to all appropriate objects, events or people.

Let's go back to our example of love. We began by recalling loving situations, loving people, loving literature, etc. We then compare all of these experiences. How are they similar? How are they different? What do some of these experiences have in common? What do the others have in common? We place them into groups and label our groups. We then proceed to use the criteria for grouping or the labels and other words from our list to synthesize our concept of love. In the future, when we are faced with new experiences, boring, hostile or loving, we store the loving experience within this conceptual framework. As you will note, concept formation is a series of processes involving recall by association, observation, comparison, classification, generalization and synthesis. No one question will promote concept formation: a series of sequential questions is required; namely, a strategy.

Traditionally, the process of concept formation has been developed via a spiral curriculum in language arts, social studies, mathematics and the sciences as well as in the fine arts. As practitioners, we are keenly aware of the fact that pupils vary in conceptual levels, so that at each grade level we have carefully selected those concepts which pupils are able to assimilate based on their abilities, level of maturation and experiential background. Our experiences have taught us that concept formation is one of the most significant processes when applied to the cognitive domain. Since the focus of this book is primarily on affective learning, I am referring you to *Effective Teaching Strategies With The Behavioral Outcomes Approach*[11], in which extensive treatment is given to concept formation at the cognitive level.

The Concept Formation At The Cognitive Level.

However, we must not lose sight of the fact that concepts have affective as well as cognitive dimensions. In teaching for concept development, we should be focusing on both dimensions. We have only to view our experiences in the past decade to be vividly reminded of the affective components of concepts such as war, peace, law and order, poverty, the separation of powers, the energy crisis, pollution, racial equality etc. In this age of television, the affective components of these concepts have been dramatically portrayed—the real drama of war, poverty, violence, peace marches, power plays and dishonesty in government have been brought right into our living rooms. We are there; the concepts are not mere words or paragraphs in a newspaper or book, but are seen in the context of real people grappling with real concerns and issues, and fighting for real values. The affective components are televised and their relevant impact is felt. But relevant concepts need not be conveyed only by television. Our schools can convey this relevancy as well. We have no need to search for relevant concepts: we have them. We have only to develop them and enlarge them in terms of their affective dimensions as well

11. Muriel Gerhard, *Effective Teaching Strategies With The Behavioral Outcomes Approach*, West Nyack, N.Y.: Parker Publishing Co., Inc., 1971.

as their cognitive dimensions. When pupils are provided with opportunities to process significant concepts on both the thought and feeling level, these concepts regain their relevancy. Cognition and affect must be combined; *both* must be utilized for the emergence of relevancy. The strategy which follows is designed to promote concept formation and is applicable to both domains.

Strategy For Concept Formation in Both The Cognitive and Affective Domains

Basic Structures:

- List all of the things, ideas, feelings, etc. you associate with _____.

- Compare the items on your list. How are they similar? How are they different?

- Place these items into two or more groups and label these groups.

- Review your groupings and items. Are there other ways in which you could group these items?

- Provided with a set of items, select those which fit your classification system and slot them into those groups.

- Using your group labels and any items within your groups, synthesize your concept of _____.

Expanding The Pupil's Concepts

In reviewing the basic structures of concept formation, you will note that the teacher provides a set of items for pupils to place or categorize within the classification system they have constructed. Our purpose here is to provide inputs to enable the pupil to expand and clarify his conceptual framework. Some of the items which we provide distinctly do not belong, but they serve a very important function. They provide both pupil and teacher with feedback to determine whether any misconceptions are held. Let's illustrate the application of the strategy of concept formation briefly to the cognitive domain and more extensively to the affective domain.

Applying The Strategy of Concept Formation to The Cognitive Domain

Let's assume we are working with second grade pupils on the concept of living things. We would begin by asking the pupils to list all of the things that come to their minds when they think of living things. The usual associations follow.

The list is by no means exhaustive.

Me	Birds	Cows
Dogs	Fish	Alligators
Cats	Turtles	Insects
Snakes	People	Monkeys
Bugs	Frogs	Gorillas
Lizards	Squirrels	Whales
Rats	Bears	Gerbils
Bees	Elephants	

We then proceed to ask the pupils to compare them and tell us how we could put them into groups. The number and kinds of groups vary. Pupils come up with classification headings such as living things which live on land, those which live on water, those who are smart and learn things, those who aren't too smart or we don't really know, those which have fur, those which don't, those who swim, those who fly, those who crawl, those with legs, those with no legs, etc. All classification systems which are valid are acceptable. Pupils find they are able to group and regroup based on their criteria. We then proceed to give them other items. Such items may include trees, flowers, plants, germs, rocks, cars, machines, etc. Pupils are asked to see which ones they can include in their groups and which ones are nonliving. Having completed this step they are then asked to list all of the things we can say about living things, in sum they are synthesizing from the available data—from their inputs and our inputs—a rather extensive summary of what we know about living things. At this point, we do not attempt to achieve closure, for we find that questions galore about living things have been asked and the pupils may decide on those questions which they would like to explore further. Exploration begins and the concept of living things and its numerous subconcepts is expanded as interest grows. You have only to apply this strategy in your classroom to appreciate its effectiveness. The pupils come alive!

Applying the Strategy of Concept Formation
To the Affective Domain

Let's assume we are working with fifth grade pupils on the concept of friendship. We would begin by asking the pupils to list all of the things that come to their minds when they think of friendship. They are to consider feelings, beliefs, attitudes, values and behaviors. Pupils are then asked to read their associations aloud and they are listed on the blackboard. A sample of some of these associations follows:

liking someone

someone who likes you

helping someone

caring

trusting

sharing

having fun together

working together

believing in someone

talking and listening

someone I value

someone I'll make sacrifices for

someone I can go to when I'm in trouble

someone who won't rat on me

people who understand me

people who don't mind my faults

kids I spend my time with because I want to

kids who enjoy the same things I do

someone who helps you but doesn't want something back

people who encourage you

people I can tell my secrets to

people who won't hurt me

kids I can tell my feelings to

people I can go to when I feel lonely and who make me feel better

kids who stick with me when I am in trouble

people I am not afraid to talk to

kids who care about the same things I do

kids I admire because they can do things I can't

We then proceed to ask the pupils to compare these items and put them into groups and label each group. Classification headings such as the following are common: sharing values, sharing interests, doing things together, sharing problems, understanding each other, caring and sacrificing, trusting and helping. Pupils discuss their headings and explore possiblities of regrouping any of the items. We then proceed to give them a list of other items. Such items may include feelings, beliefs, attitudes, values and behaviors: you can't trust anyone; most people are basically good; I'll help you if you help me; How could you do that! I'll give you this record in exchange for _____; Sure, I'll listen, tell me all about it; Come on, let's get a soda, you'll feel better if you stop worrying; You can do it, I know you can! I know how you feel, everybody feels that way once in a while; That's great, let's do something special; You've got to see my new bike and try it. Pupils are asked to determine which of these items they can include in their groups and which do not belong in any category. Having completed this step, they are asked to summarize all of the items to come up with their idea of friendship. Again, we do not attempt to achieve any permanent closure. Pupils may decide to explore the concept further, to collect quotations, proverbs and poems, and write short case studies of friendly and unfriendly behaviors which other pupils in the class may analyze. They may decide to put together a book on friendship, with songs, artwork and photographs depicting feelings, beliefs, values and behaviors which illustrate this concept. Affective classroom experiences such as these stimulate further affective behavior.

Summary

The process skills which we have dealt with in this chapter and Chapters 3 and 4 will achieve the major goals of affective development. Our pupils will be provided with skills whose relevancy they will not question. They will practice them and apply them to the most relevant curriculum they possess—their lives.

6

How To Begin Specifying Objectives in the Affective Domain

Updating Our Progress

Let's review our progress up to this point. In Chapter 1 a new blueprint for education was proposed and outlined—one which would restore the much needed relevancy to education. This blueprint encompasses the following six major components or concerns:

- The promotion of affective growth
- The development of highly cognitive skills
- A modification of curriculum resulting in a "balanced" affective-cognitive curruculum
- The development of teaching competencies in both domains
- The implementation of an instructional system that individualizes cognitively and affectively, allowing for the growth of the total individual
- The development of a strong and positive self-concept in pupils resulting in autonomous individuals capable of coping successfully with the unpredictable demands of the future.

In Chapter 2 we have dealt with self-concept in very concrete terms—as a sense of self-worth, an ability to cope, an ability for affective expression and a sense of autonomy. We focused on how all of these senses and abilities were interrelated and how self-concept affected motivation, discipline and most importantly learning. We explored the new generation's search for "role" as well as "goal" and the extremely significant impact and implications of this search on educational practice. Our role as teachers and administrators in creating a responsive environment—one which would realistically promote role and goal development—was spelled out in detail. The Behavioral Outcomes Approach in its expanded format, utilizing the, *process skills* not only in the cognitive but in the *affective domain,* was detailed in Chapters 3, 4 and 5. The major process skills, their operational definitions, the rationale for their use in both domains, questioning techniques, step-by-step strategies and their sample applications to personal and curricular content were provided for direct classroom use.

Integrating Affective Goals and
Objectives Into The Curriculum

Our next step is to integrate these affective skills and strategies into our existing curriculum so that we do indeed achieve a "balanced" whole. Those of us who have been involved in curriculum modification and adaptation know all too well that haphazard "tacking-on" is not the answer. For a variety of reasons, these "tacked-on" modifications are short-lived and temporary. In far too many cases, they have *not* been incorporated into the goals and objectives of the total school system. They are usually initiated as "pilot" programs in "pilot" schools with "pilot" grant funds. The pilot light goes out when these funds run out. Unless the school system has the leadership, commitment and local funds to continue the program to disseminate the program to the system as a whole, the program dies. In other cases, a pilot program in its initial stages, has been diffused throughout the school system. The leadership has imbedded the program's goals and objectives into the total school system's goals and objectives, modified these goals and objectives and reassessed their priorities. The old is stripped away and the new remains and grows. All of us have either experienced or read about examples of both kinds of cases.

If we are committed to the task of integrating affect with cognition, to create a "balanced" and relevant curriculum, our first and major step is to identify our affective goals and then proceed to translate these goals into realistic, viable and feasible affective objectives—objectives which are so stated that they clearly communicate their intent and can be readily implemented by the classroom teacher. The days of grandiose goals and objectives couched in impressive, but not very expressive pedaguese, are over! Within the past decade, the message has been emphatically reinforced. We have only to examine the "words of the decade"—behavioral objectives, performance objectives, measurable objectives, mastery levels, minimum levels of acceptable performance, entry behaviors, diagnosis, pre-testing, post testing and accountability—to become fully cognizant that as educators, we are being asked to specify in concrete, realistic terms precisely what our pupils will be able to achieve at specific levels of the educative process and how we will be able to evaluate these achievements.

Objectives—"New" and Improved

As educators we will all agree that the concept of specifying objectives is by no means new. To use the cliche—"Yes, we have always had objectives." The major difference between the past and the present is simply that "in those days" we had them "in mind." When we put them in writing, they were inserted in the old-fashioned lesson plan book under the purpose of our lesson. In 99.9 percent of the cases, the objective made no mention of the pupil. We rarely, if ever, stated that "the pupil will be able to _____ as measured by _____." In 99.9 percent of the cases, the objective was a teacher-centered objective or a "to whom it may concern" objective—"to investigate the properties of matter." In most cases, the list of objectives, when reviewed for their sequential pattern, merely reflected the sequence of the specific text being used and had little or nothing to do with a logical learning sequence in terms of the specific groups of pupils being taught and their diagnosed needs. The text was taught and covered. As for the pupils, well, we assumed that they too were taught and covered! The worth of those objectives as well as the old-fashioned plan book is indeed questionable. But we have come a long way in terms of objectives. We are no longer content to have our objectives "in mind." School systems and textbook publishers are specifying pupil objectives in behavioral terms, in performance terms, in measurable terms. Teachers and aministrators are spending endless hours in determining realistic mastery levels for their specific groups of pupils. Criterion-referenced tests are being constructed so that we are testing for what we have taught.

But, as always, there are those who still question the need for specifying pupil objectives in behavioral terms: there are those who still are critical of behavioral objectives, expressing the view that the *most significant objectives* cannot be stated in behavioral and measurable terms, and that these objectives—the highly cognitive objectives, the essential affective objectives—are intangible and defy measurement. "It can't be done!" they say. As long as they hold this mind set and perceive this task as impossible, it will not be done! In actuality, it can be done and is being done. How it is done will be dealt with in this chapter and Chapter 7.

Reassessing The Practical Worth of Goals and Objectives

But let's stop for a moment and reassess the entire concept of establishing goals and writing objectives. In serving as a consultant to school systems, I have frequently found that the central office administrative staff is determined to take the objectives route but has failed to clearly communicate to principals and teachers the personal value of these objectives. The principals and teachers do not understand the usefulness of this tool and how it will make their jobs easier. To many, it is just somebody's bright idea with which they are burdened and which they must implement.

Let's start with the indisputable premise that education is a purposeful process. Its purposes are expressed in global terms as goals. As the major vehicles of education, school systems have identified their goals. A typical listing may include most of the following goals: Pupils will be provided with:

- Knowledge—concepts, generalizations, principles and specific data of the major disciplines.
- Tool Skills
  a. Basic Skills—reading, writing and computation
  b. Specific Skills—using a ruler, protractor, slide rule, microscope, etc.
- Cognitive or "Problem-Solving" Skills—using process skills such as observation, comparision, classification, and inductive and deductive reasoning
- Opportunities To Develop a Positive Self-Concept
- Opportunities To Become Self-Directive
- Opportunities To Become Socially Effective
- Opportunities To Develop Positive Attitudes and Values Toward Schooling and Education

We cannot argue with these goals. They do provide a broad overview of the purposes of schools and that is their function. But for the school administrator, the classroom teacher, the pupil, the parent and members of the community they are inadequate. For all of us to operate, understand, communicate and value the process of education: they must be translated into down-to-earth specifics.

As a teacher, let's say of an ecology course or a mathematics course, to be told that I must provide my pupils with a basic knowledge, understanding and appreciation of ecology or mathematics tells me little. My first question is "Where is the curriculum?" or, translated into an operational question: "What knowledge, understanding and appreciations do you want my pupils to demonstrate?"

As a parent, to be told at a PTA meeting that my child is taking a basic course in ecology or mathematics tells me little. Today's parent will ask his child for the textbook and peruse it to find out what Johnny is learning in school. As a pupil, the same message conveys little if anything at all. However, if each of us is provided with a listing of the *major* specific objectives, namely, what key concepts, basic principles and skills the pupil should master in this course, then all of us are able to function positively and constructively in our specific role. Identifying precisely what the pupil should be able to do as a result of this course tells the teacher specifically what knowledge and skills to teach, tells the pupil what he is responsible for as a learner and enables the parent to acquire a comprehensive picture of the school's curriculum.

In sum, translating disciplines to a sequential listing of the *major* specific objectives provides an instructional road map for the teacher, a learning map for the pupil and a communications map for the parents and the community.

The Status of Objectives

To date, increasing numbers of school systems have recognized that the specification of objectives is an invaluable tool for the purposes of systematic instruction and evaluation. The majority of school systems have focused on the conventional basic skills areas such as reading, writing and computation. Others have provided cadres of teachers with released time to specify objectives in the traditional disciplines such as social studies, language arts, the sciences, art, music, etc. Still others have recognized the need for promoting highly cognitive skills, moving beyond mere rote memorization and recall to process skills such as induction, analysis, synthesis and critical thinking. Still others are concerned with affective behaviors, recognizing their direct impact on cognitive learning and their pupil's needs for self-actualization. It is in this area that teachers are encountering difficulties in spelling out what the pupil will be able to do, what overt behaviors will be demonstrated and how these will be measured. In this chapter, therefore, we will focus on affective goals and affective behavioral objectives.

Obtaining A Working Knowledge of Affective Objectives

In practice, I have found that the most effective, efficient and satisfying way of providing teachers and administrators with a working knowledge of writing objectives is to provide them with the opportunity to do just that—work with objectives and *experience* all of the basic skills and understanding in a sequential manner until, lo and behold, they then find that they have attained their objective. Our focus is on the construction of affective objectives, for our purpose is to integrate these objectives into the current cognitive curricula so that our schools attain a "balanced" affective-cognitive curriculum.

For those who have had minimal exposure to the actual writing of objectives, or have used commercially prepared objectives, it is essential to become well acquainted with the general guidelines in writing objectives. In addition, it is important to become familiar with the language of objectives. In the working papers that follow, you will be amazed at how simple the task is once you acquire the terminology and understand the purposes.

General Guidelines In Writing Objectives

1. In writing objectives, you are focusing on the pupil. *The objective is a pupil objective.* It states as precisely as possible—what the pupil will be able to do or demonstrate as a result of one or more learning activities. It states the pupil *outcome*—the result—the *ends* in terms of how the pupil will *behave.* Many of us have thought of the term "behavioral outcomes" as synonomous with "behavioral objective." Our purpose is to change the pupil's behavior in some way. By changing his behavior, we mean a variety of things: if he can't count by twos and then he can do so as a result of a series of instructional activities, his behavior has changed. If he comes to class hating books and then begins to take an interest in them, his behavior has changed. We are not speaking of behavior in the context of discipline; we are focusing on his ac-

tions, reactions and interactions in all of its aspects—not simply whether he disciplines himself in class and adheres to the school's rules and regulations.

2. In writing objectives, we are focusing on *outcomes—ends, not means.* We are *not incorporating the instructional methodology* that is to be used by the teacher to assist the pupil in achieving the changed behavior. We are not dictating to our colleagues how they will teach the child to count by twos, add, subtract or multiply. We are merely stating what the *end result* will be. As professionals working with diverse pupil populations, the selection of instructional means is left to us. Too often teachers and administrators, with the best intentions in mind, construct objectives and incorporate materials and methodology. They have not only missed the boat, but serve to alienate their colleagues. I can't help thinking of the fourth grade pupil who wrote a very short composition on Socrates. "Socrates," she wrote, "was a great Greek philosopher. He gave advice. They poisoned him!" The objective is a statement describing the pupil outcome and should be limited to that! We are not giving advice or dictating methodology to our colleagues. *What we are doing is establishing basic uniformity and agreement as to what our pupils should achieve.*

3. In writing objectives, we are attempting to use *words that clearly communicate the same meaning to all*—words that have very concrete meanings and are not open to diverse interpretations. In all cases *where it is possible,* we select words that denote a *readily observable* behavior. Words such as writes, describes, counts, constructs, recites, discusses, identifies, and names do denote observable behaviors. However, were we to use words such as understands, comprehends, really understands, grasps the significance of, develop the concept of, we find that they do not denote an observable behavior. How do you and I "know" that the child really understands? No light goes on; no buzzer buzzes. Therefore, we avoid those words wherever possible.

4. In writing objectives, we are not only concerned with stating clearly what the pupil will be able to do, but how we will be able to *measure* or determine that he can indeed to it. The very realistic factor of measurability is introduced. Our objective should state not only what he will be able to do but also how it will be measured. For example: the pupil will be able to spell the words on X list correctly as measured by a written test. In short, our objective should include the *pupil outcome and how it will be measured.* As we will discover in constructing affective objectives, the process of measuring may not be direct, but *indirect.* When we are dealing with the pupil's self-concept, feelings, attitudes, in-

terests and appreciations, direct measurement is not always possible, so we search for as many *indicators* as we can gather to determine how he feels about himself and others, whether he really enjoys reading or mathematics or science, whether he really appreciates certain forms of art or music. The fact that these objectives are not directly and readily measurable should not cause us to delete them from the school curriculum. The additional effort is certainly worthy of the result—affective growth and maturity.

5. In writing objectives, teachers are frequently concerned with the *level* of *specificity*. How specific, how detailed should the objective be? The answer, my friends, rests with you. If your purpose is to have the pupils enjoy square dancing, that is it. You will not list every step of the square dance; you will not measure each pupil to determine whether he has "perfected" each step. You simply want him to enjoy it, participate in it, and go to square dances when they are announced. Too often teachers have read books and articles on writing objectives and feel they have to follow the recipes to a T. Let's do away with that misconception. We modify the recipe based on our own purposes and needs.

Utilizing Working Papers

Given these five guidelines—the objective is a pupil objective; it focuses on ends or outcomes, not means or methods; it is couched in clear terms; it specifies methods of measurement, direct or indirect ones, and is as specific as the purposes and needs dictate—we are ready to begin to utilize the working papers. Each working paper has a general format. We are given the objective, a semantic guide which defines our terms so that we are all speaking the same language and assigning the same meaning to specific terms, criterion questions which serve to assist us in same meaning to specific terms, criterion questions which serve to assist us in responding to the exercises, and directions for each exercise and feedback on our responses. The feedback may be simply a listing of the "right" answers, in many cases with a brief explanation of why they are "right."

To provide an overview of the skills and sequence of skills we will become involved with, the following listing of working papers is given:

Working Paper #1—*Affective Goals vs. Affective Objectives*—What is the difference between an affective goal and an affective objective?

Working Paper #2—Designating Behaviors—What constitutes a behavior?

Working Paper #3—*Overt vs. Covert Behaviors*—How do we determine whether a behavior is overt or covert for practical purposes?

Working Paper #4—*Unmixing the Behavioral Mix*—Recognizing that most behaviors are a mix of cognitive, affective and psychomotor components, how do we classify them into the three domains for practical purposes?

Working Paper #5—*Operational Terminology For Affective Description*—How precise can our terminology be in writing affective objectives?

Working Paper #6—*Performance Objectives in the Affective Domain*—How important if performance in the affective domain?

Working Paper #7—*Measurability in the Affective Domain*—How do we identify indirect methods of measurement for affective objectives?

Discussion Paper #8—*Affective Mastery Levels*—Should we specify "mastery levels" in the affective domain? If so, on what basis? If not, why not?

Working Paper #9—*Matching Affective Objectives With Affective "Tests"*—How can we "test" for affective growth without stifling that growth or reducing affective learning to a game of "Feeling Right and Valuing Right"?

In this chapter, we will deal with working papers #1 through #5. In Chapter 7, *"Completing the Construction of Affective Objectives,"* we will focus in greater detail on the evaluation of affective objectives, using working papers and discussion papers #6 through #9.

Let's begin with working paper #1, in which we eliminate the confusion of using goals and objectives interchangeably and view each one as a distinct entity serving its own purpose.

Working Paper #1
Affective Goals vs. Affective Objectives

Objective: Given a semantic guide and a set of criterion questions, we will be able to differentiate between an affective goal and an affective objective. This will be measured by using a written form.

Semantic Guide:

Affective Goal—a *very general statement open to many interpretations* dealing with the pupils' feelings, emotions, attitudes, beliefs, values interests and appreciation.

Affective Objective—description, clearly stating what the learner will be able to demonstrate as a result of a series of affective learning experiences and how this will be measured.

Criterion Questions:

The critical questions which a properly stated affective objective answers are:

1. Does it *state* what the pupil will be able to do or demonstrate *specifically* so that we, the teachers, have no need to interpret any part of this statement?

2. Does it state how we, the teachers, will determine whether the pupil has achieved this affective objective? Will we be able to observe the outcome directly? Will we use teacher-made "tests"? Will we analyze pupil-produced products such as brief descriptions, stories, essays, poems and art forms? Will we employ "before and after" inventories or questionnaires to assess behavioral change indirectly? Will we review pupil's open diaries?

If the answers to these criterion questions are yes, the statement is an objective. If the answers are no and the statement is global or general, *devoid of any means of measurement,* the statement is a goal. This is not to say that goals are bad or that objectives are good. What we are saying is that golas map the general area of behavior and objectives pinpoint the specific behavior or sets of behaviors and their means of measurement.

Directions: Read each of the following statements. Analyze them in terms of the criterion questions. In the blanks preceeding each statement, designate those statements which are affective goals by using the letters *AG* and those which are affective objectives by using the letters *AO*.

The pupil will:

_____ 1. develop a strong, positive self-concept.

_____ 2. become a more independent individual.

_____ 3. demonstrate increased self-direction.

_____ 4. develop an appreciation for schooling and education.

_____ 5. become socially effective.

_____ 6. become more open in the exploration and expression of his own feelings by describing them freely in classroom discussions, in role-playing situations and in products such as stories, poems and art forms.

_____ 7. demonstrate a sense of self-worth by describing the characteristics which make him a special and unique individual.

_____   8.   demonstrate confidence in dealing with new situations, new people and new issues by entering freely into these situations, befriending and interacting with newcomers and expressing his opinions and concerns in regard to new issues with little or no hesitation.

_____   9.   value and respect others by listening to others attentively, assisting them when help is needed, replying tactfully and positively in conversations, and sharing and cooperating in group activities.

_____   10. assume greater responsibility for himself by completing the tasks he has accepted, by demonstrating greater effort to improve, by increasing participation in personally relevant activities and by accepting the blame or consequences when commitments are not met.

Feedback

In this exercise items 1, 2, 3, 4 and 5 are all affective goals. They describe general behaviors or sets of behaviors. We are not told specifically what constitutes a strong, positive self-concept, what a more independent individual is or does, what behaviors constitute increased self-direction or an appreciation for schooling or education, or what being socially effective means in behavioral terms. As classroom teachers, we would of necessity have to interpret each of them and list the behaviors for which we would instruct and by which we would assess growth or change. Items 6, 7, 8, 9 and 10 are affective objectives: they start out in general terms *but* proceed to spell out in each case the *behaviors* or *products* by which we can *measure* whether the objective is being attained.

For example, in item 6, the pupil will become more open in the exploration and expression of his own feelings. How do we determine this? The statement goes on to answer the question—by describing these feelings freely in classroom discussions (we do not have to prod the pupil, nor would we!), by free expression in role-playing situations and in pupil-produced products such as stories, poems and art forms. In the case of these products, we would have to analyze them carefully to determine whether free expression or "game" expression is going on.

In item 7, the pupil will demonstrate his sense of self-worth. The question, "How will he do this?" is answered for us. He will describe the characteristics which he perceives as making him a special and unique individual. Therefore, at this time, he provides me with a self-profile. Whether I see him in this manner does not matter; I accept his perception. Later on in the year, I may repeat this activity and compare the early and later profiles and use them in conjunction with my daily classroom observations to determine whether his sense of self-worth is maintained or growing.

In item 8, I am concerned with the pupil's development of confidence in dealing with new situations, people and issues. The key question again arises, "How do I measure the pupil's confidence?" The objective provides me with the method of measurement. I observe for specific behaviors, namely, the pupil enters *freely* into these situations; he befriends and interacts with newcomers in the classroom; when confronted with new issues, he expresses his opinions and concerns rather than remaining silent or waiting for me to call upon him.

In item 9, the statement again begins in a general vein, but proceeds to spell out for me what valuing and respecting others mean in terms of specific behaviors. If we or our pupils value and respect others, we do listen to them attentively, we do offer to assist them when we sense that help is needed, we do reply tactfully and positively, and we share and cooperate with others. We may exhibit many other positive behaviors—but this objective as stated does communicate to us what valuing and respecting others means and what we are to look for in measuring its occurrence.

In item 10, the statement is obviously an objective. We are told in behavioral terms what constitutes greater responsibility for oneself. We know what behaviors to look for to measure its occurrence.

In sum, differentiating between an affective goal and an affective objective is an easy task. The goal statement is general; the objective statement may be initially general but is expanded to break down the general and provide us with specific behaviors for which to instruct and by which to measure.

Designating Behaviors

Let's proceed with working paper #2—*Designating Behaviors*. To date, considerable confusion has resulted from the diverse ways by which the term behavior has been defined and used. Some have used behavior as denoting *only observable behavior*. This is a misuse of the term. A behavior is any action, reaction or interaction on the part of an organism. It may be either observable (overt) or nonobservable (covert). The critics of behavioral objectives, accepting the popular definition of "only observable behavior" have dramatically pointed out that numerous critical "behaviors" are nonobservable—and they are right! To limit behavior to observable action is to subtract half of our being. For example, when we as teachers are suddenly provided with an additional new program to be implemented within an already tight schedule, we may and do experience considerable anxiety. Some of us may express that anxiety by speaking with our colleagues and venting our feelings; others may sit in that teacher's room experiencing future educational shock but saying nothing. Experiencing the anxiety is certainly a behavior. Sitting there stunned is certainly a behavior. Taking overt action *or* refraining from overt action are both behaviors. In basic psychology courses we have classified behaviors as overt and covert. This is as it should be. There is not practical need to distort the meaning of the term. We have merely to use the proper adjective overt or covert. Based on this preliminary introduction, you should experience no difficulty in completing working paper #2 which follows.

Working Paper #2
Designating Behaviors
Objective: Given a semantic guide, you will be able to identify those statements which describe a behavior.

Semantic Guide:

Definition: A behavior is any action, reaction, or interaction on the part of an individual. The action may be overt (observable) or covert (nonobservable or hidden).
Directions: Examine the following statements. Applying the definition of behavior as given above, place a *B* in front of each statement which designates a behavior.

_____ 1. The pupil adds a column of two digit numbers correctly.
_____ 2. The pupil enjoys a sunset.
_____ 3. The pupil describes his reaction to the book "Jaws."
_____ 4. The pupil appreciates a musical recording.
_____ 5. The pupil worries about his grades.

_____ 6. The weather is cold.

_____ 7. The pupil values friends.

_____ 8. The pupil enjoys the humor of a situation.

_____ 9. The leaves are red.

_____ 10. The pupil is interested in computers.

_____ 11. The pupil constructs a diorama.

_____ 12. The pupil demonstrates how to use a siphon.

Feedback: Statements 1, 2, 3, 4, 5, 7, 8, 10, 11 and 12 all designate behaviors. They may differ in terms of the *kind* of behavior they are, namely overt or observable and covert or not always or not readily observable, but they are behaviors—actions, reactions or interactions—responses to stimuli. Statements 6 and 9 are merely descriptions of existing conditions and do not make mention of an individual behaving in any manner.

Overt and Covert Behaviors

In working paper #3, you will differentiate between an overt or observable behavior and a covert or nonobservable behavior. From a practical standpoint, this is very important. There are many behaviors that do not fall exclusively into one category. For example, let's deal with behaviors such as enjoys, is happy, is discouraged, tries hard. There are obviously times when these behaviors are quite apparent merely by observing specific pupils; based on our knowledge of them and our numerous contacts with them, we "know" them and can "read" them. These less tangible behaviors are then observable to us.

On the other hand, many pupils are not that transparent, do not readily display these reactions or display them in rather different ways. All of us have been confronted with "quiet" pupils who do not "show" their true feelings, who repress or suppress them, who wear the "poker" face. In these cases, enjoying, being happy, experiencing frustration and trying hard are invisible behaviors. Therefore, for practical purposes, to establish and maintain categories which are mutually exclusive, we must simply establish definite parameters. An observable behavior will be one that is always observable, such as reading aloud, discussing, writing or drawing. A nonobservable behavior will be one that is *not always* readily observable, such as enjoying, appreciating, disliking, liking, etc. With this preliminary explanation, you should experience no difficulty in responding to the exercise in working paper #3 which follows.

Working Paper #3
Differentiating Between Overt and Covert Behaviors

Objective: Given a semantic guide, you will be able to differentiate between overt and covert behaviors as measured by your responses to the following items.

Semantic Guide:

Overt Behavior: A behavior which is *observable at all times.* Examples: The pupil swims, the pupil writes, the pupil reads aloud.
Covert Behavior: A behavior which is *not readily observable at all times,* but may be hidden in some instances. Examples: The pupil is happy. The pupil is frightened. These behaviors are not *always* readily observable.

Criterion Question:

Is the behavior observable at all times? If so, it is classified as overt.
Directions: Using an *O* for overt and a *C* for covert, label the following behaviors:
The pupil:

_____ 1. listens to the teacher's directions.

_____ 2. draws two dimensional shapes such as circles, squares and triangles.

_____ 3. constructs a diorama.

_____ 4. withdraws from a threatening situation.

_____ 5. analyzes a newspaper account.

_____ 6. is interested in folk-rock.

_____ 7. is willing to take risks.

_____ 8. likes being outdoors.

_____ 9. appreciates modern art.

_____ 10. defends a cause strongly by making a dramatic speech.

Feedback: Items 2, 3 and 10 are overt behaviors. Behaviors such as drawing, constructing and defending via speechmaking are all readily observable.

Items 1, 4, 5, 6, 7, 8 and 9 are not *always* readily observable. The pupil who appears to be listening attentively may be daydreaming or recalling a T.V. program he saw last night. The pupil who in reality is withdrawing from a situation which he perceives as threatening may give the outward appearance of calmness; the pupil who is analyzing a newspaper account is using a process skill. We can only be certain that he has analyzed the account when he either verbalizes his analysis or puts it in writing. We cannot observe the process taking place.

The same holds true for items 6, 7, 8 and 9; we as teachers cannot always directly observe interest in a specific field, willingness to take risks, liking or appreciating. All too often, we have to devise or create situations in which the pupil hopefully will react and even then the individual reactions will and should differ. In sum, for our purposes, observable behaviors have the key word, *always,* preceding them and when we are confronted with "definite maybe's," we classify these behaviors as covert. Our categories in this way do become mutually exclusive.

The Behavioral Mix

In working paper #4, we are "unmixing the behavioral mix." We are confronting the reality that there are few if any behaviors that are "pure," in the sense of being purely cognitive or intellectual, purely affective or emotional and purely psychomotor or manipulative. Since the individual is a mixture of all of these domains, and although in numerous instances we do attempt to compartmentalize our intellectual thoughts, our feelings and our manual skills, in reality they are intertwined; they do interact. It is extremely rare that, as human beings, we can and do function solely in one domain. We would like to perceive ourselves as doing so but this is not the case in practice.

There are many educators who have come away with the misconception of the existence of discrete domains, as a result of their reading about the cognitive or affective domains and as a result of college courses or workshops in each of these domains. The writers of these texts, who produced excellent products, had no intent of conveying this misconception. However, the misconception persists. For instructional purposes and for clarity's sake, the domains were dealt with on an individual basis. However, with no desire to belabor the point but with every desire to clarify it, most behaviors are a mix of two or more domains.

When we analyze the mix, however, we find that in each instance, one domain dominates. For example, in a social studies class-

)

room, we may be identifying the major conditions which prompted us to enter into the Viet Nam War. The focus is on the cognitive; however, in our discussion, affective components will certainly enter the picture and will be heard. This is as it should be. Our objective— the pupil will be able to identify at least two of the major conditions which prompted U.S. entrance into the Viet Nam War—would be classified as *highly* cognitive. However, if we were to change the objective to—the pupil will be given the opportunity to discuss the diversity of feelings and attitudes people held about our involvement in Viet Nam—our objective is now *highly* affective. Yes, we start from a factual base, but we proceed to an exploration of feelings and attitudinal sets. Therefore, in order to achieve one of our goals, the creation of a "balanced" cognitive-affective curriculum, it is essential that we are able to classify our objectives as highly cognitive or highly affective or highly psychomotor. By using the word *highly,* we constantly remind ourselves that "pure" rarely exists, that the mix does, and that the classification system is an essential tool to develop the "balanced" curriculum or mix.

In working paper #4 which follows, again you should experience little difficulty in classifying objectives as highly cognitive, highly affective and highly psychomotor.

Working Paper #4
"Unmixing the Behavioral Mix"

Objective: Given a list of behavioral objectives, you will be able to identify those which are highly cognitive, highly affective and highly psychomotor.

Semantic Guide:

Cognitive Behaviors	—deals with process skills applied to factual data, focusing on concepts, principles and generalizations in the knowledge area.
Affective Behaviors	—deals with the exploration and expression of feelings, emotions, beliefs, attitudes, values, interests and appreciations.
Psychomotor Behaviors	—deals with physical neuromuscular and manipulative skills such as working with a saw, using a typewriter, operating a sewing machine, learning to swim, etc.

Criterion Question:

Focusing on the first part of the objective (the stem), in which domain is the *emphasis* placed (thinking or cognitive, emotive or affective, manipulative or psychomotor)?

Directions: Examine the following behaviors. Use a *C* for those which you view as *highly* cognitive, and *A* for those which you view as *highly* affective and a *P* for those which are *highly* psychomotor. How the objective is *stated* will determine your response.

_____ 1. The pupil lists the names of three plays written by Eugene O'Neill and describes their major themes.

_____ 2. The pupil selects one of the plays written by Eugene O'Neill which has personal significance to him and describes his feelings, interest in and appreciation of the play.

_____ 3. The pupil listens attentively to his classmates' diverse interpretations of a play and verbally concludes that people differ in their perceptions and views and should be respected for these differences.

_____ 4. The pupil demonstrates his knowledge of the basic principles of simple machines by applying this knowledge and constructing three simple machines.

_____ 5. The pupil demonstrates improved skill in typing by increasing his rate from 40 to 60 words per minute without making an error.

_____ 6. The pupil demonstrates his interest in ecology by organizing an ecology club, obtaining a teacher sponsor, recruiting participants, and giving of his time on weekends to improve the school grounds.

_____ 7. Having researched the issue of mercy killing, the pupil presents the data to the class, describes his stand on the issue, defends his stand and attempts to persuade others to support him.

_____ 8. Having compared a variety of living and non-living things, the pupil states their similarities and differences and states his definition of "being."

Feedback:

Items 1, 4 and 8 are highly cognitive behaviors. In item 1 the pupil operates on a cognitive level by recalling the names of the plays and describing their themes. Although the level of cognition is merely recall, the behavior is cognitive. Few of us as teachers would limit instruction in literature to this level. Most of us would use it as the initial base from which to build interpretive and analytical skills.

In item 4, the behavior is highly cognitive. The pupil having learned the basic principles of simple machines is now demonstrating his knowledge in the most practical sense—that of applying it—by constructing three simple machines. We are not concerned with his *skills of construction*. We are concerned with his "comprehension" of the principles. If he can put them to work by actually applying them, then he "really understands" these basic principles. No, this is not a psychomotor skill. If we reread statement #4, the stem of the statement clearly tells us we are concerned with his *knowledge* of the basic principles of simple machines and we are *measuring the mastery of this knowledge* by his application of the knowledge in the form of constructing three machines.

In item 8, the behavior is highly cognitive. The pupil is applying process skills such as observation, comparision and synthesis to "factual" data or phenomena, namely, living and non-living things and abstracting from the data the essence of "living."

Now when we review items 2, 3, 6 and 7 we find that they are all highly affective. By no means are they totally affective. The cognitive-affective mix is highly apparent in items 2, 3 and 7. In items 2 and 3 the pupil starts from a cognitive base—he has read the plays—but in item 2 the focus is on his personal reaction. He is asked to describe the *personal meaning* the play has for him, his feelings, his own interest in and what aspects he appreciates.

In item 3, the focus again is on affect; the pupil realizes and respects the fact that individuals differ in and are entitled to their own perceptions and views.

In item 6, the cognitive base is merely inferred, for an interest in ecology usually stems from some knowledge of ecology and its problems. The pupil may not necessarily have an extensive knowledge but just enough to activate interest. Item 6 is highly affective. The pupil's interest in and valuing of sound ecological practices is demonstrated by his actions.

In item 7, we again have the mix, but the pupil moves from the cognitive data to *personal involvement* with the issue attempting to present a strong case for his view and to gather the support of his classmates.

Item 5 is highly psychomotor. Yes, the cognitive base is there in terms of the essential rote skills of spelling and punctuation, but the skill of correct and efficient use of the typewriter is the focus.

In sum, what we are discovering is that there is always a mix. What is essential for our purposes is to determine whether the *key ingredients* are affective, cognitive or psychomotor.

Clear-Cut Terminology in the Affective Domain

In working paper #5, we will be dealing with the major problem posed by the ciritcs of behavioral objectives—that of using clear-cut terminology for describing affective behaviors. If you will recall guideline number 3, emphasis was placed on using words that clearly communicate the same meaning to all, using words that have very concrete meanings and are not open to diverse interpretations. Our choice of words *whenever possible* was to include terms that denote *readily observable behaviors.* Readily observable behaviors provide us with directly and *readily measurable behaviors.* This is fine. We favored words such as writes, describes, constructs, states, and draws. We avoided words such as understands, comprehends, grasps the significance of or develops the concept of. These ambiguous words can be avoided in many instances.

For example, let's assume that we have come across a poorly stated objective which reads: The pupil will "comprehend" Boyle's Law. We are confronted with the problem of how do we measure for "comprehends" Boyle's Law. It is far more practical to simply rewrite the objective to read: The pupil will state Boyle's Law and cite two examples of its practical application. As the teacher, I can then readily measure his "comprehension" of Boyle's Law: he can *state the law* and he can *cite two examples of its use.* Therefore the practical value of using clear terminology is obvious. If we are able to state the objective in terms that denote readily observable and readily measurable behaviors, why not!

But in the affective domain, we are confronted with a problem. We are not *directly* dealing with tangible skills such as reading, writing, computation, and verbalizations of data; we are dealing with feelings, emotions, attitudes, interests, appreciations and values. We want the pupil to develop an interest in reading, to appreciate himself, others, the arts, the sciences, and the humanities; to value, and to display specific attitudinal sets toward his peers, his education, his parents, his environment. Obviously these words—feels, is interested in, enjoys, appreciates, values—are not *clear* terms: *they do not denote readily observable and directly measurable behaviors.* I cannot help but recall an incident where I reported on the results of a study stating that there was increased teacher satisfaction. The question raised was simply, "How did you measure it, by the length of the teacher's smile?"

Are we really at a loss for words? Not at all. As educators, we are practical and flexible people, and practical and flexible people do not attempt to put square pegs into round holes or toss aside those square pegs when they are vital and significant educational objectives. Flexibility is the answer. What we are searching for in the *writing of affective objectives* are *operational terms,* terms that will enable us to describe these vital and critical affective objectives and terms that will pinpoint how we can measure these intangibles *indirectly*. This is where our flexibility enters; we will *combine* the ambiguous terms with the clear terms, keeping in mind that our purpose is to construct affective objectives with which we can operate and which communicate the same message to all of us.

For example, let's reassess an affective objective which we used earlier in this chapter. The pupil will value and respect others by listening to others attentively, assisting them when help is needed, replying tactfully and positively in conversations and discussions, and sharing and cooperating in group activities. What is our objective? That the pupil learn to value and respect others. How do we measure it? By observing—by looking for specific behaviors which are listed in the objective which would *indicate* that the pupil does value and respect others. Does he listen attentively to others? Does he offer assistance to others? Is he tactful and positive in his interactions with others? Does he share? Does he work cooperatively with his peers? Do we as teachers all understand what the objective is and how we are to measure for its attainment? Was our "mixed" terminology operational? Indeed it was. Therefore we can conclude that in writing objectives which are affective, we will begin our objective by using "ambiguous" terminology as the stem of the statement and then proceed to make it operational by citing the specific behaviors which will serve as *indicators* by which we can measure the attainment of the objective. The greater the number of pertinent indicators, the greater validity our measurements will have!

If there is one thing we as teachers have learned in our classrooms, it is to be realistic. In dealing with feelings, emotions, attitudes, beliefs, interests, appreciations and values, we are involved with the inner space and inner lives of our pupils, not with concrete surface skills; therefore, a simple description is inadequate. The fact that an operational description requires more effort will certainly not deter us. Our commitment to the development of the total child is total!

Working Paper #5
Operational Terminology For Affective Description

Objective: Given a semantic guide, you will be able to state affective objectives in operational terms by identifying the behaviors and/or products which demonstrate that the objective can be measured and therefore has been attained.

Our Semantic Guide:

An Operational Definition is one that describes what the individual *does* and/or *observes*.

For example, let's operationalize the objective: The pupil values friendship. How do we "know" he values friendship? He behaves in friendly ways. What are "friendly ways?" He seeks out those of his peers with whom he wants to develop friendships. He shares activities and possessions with them. He talks and confides with them. He lunches with them. He listens to them. He assists them. He shows concern about their feelings and thoughts. He defends them. All of these behaviors are *indicators* of valuing friendship and are descriptions of "friendly ways." We can observe them if we *look* for them. Therefore in writing our objective we would combine all of these behaviors. Our objective would read: The pupil values friendship as demonstrated by the following behavioral indicators:

    a. he seeks out others.
    b. he shares activities and possessions with them.
    c. he talks with and confides in them.
    d. he assists them.
    e. he listens to them.
    f. he verbally shows concern in regard to their feelings and thoughts
    g. he defends them.

We have operationalized "valuing friendship". Another method of operationalizing is that of using a pupil-product.
A Product—something the pupil produces: an account, a story, a poem, an essay, responses on an inventory or a questionnaire, or a verbal statement which *substantiates* the affective behavior.

For example, let's continue with the same affective objective: The pupil values friendship. The products which may substantiate this could be a poem he writes on friendship, an essay on the value of friends, a story whose lesson stresses the meaning of friendship, responses on an inventory which clearly indicate that he values friends as opposed to being a loner. Therefore, our operational affective objective may consist of pupil-produced products, as well as behaviors, which indicate that he values friendship.

Directions: Below you will find a series of incomplete affective objectives and a set of *behaviors* and *product* which serve to operationalize these objectives. Check only those which you consider to be appropriate to complete the objective and which provide you with a valid means of measuring its attainment.

1. The pupil demonstrates an interest in the current political scene as measured by

   _____ a. his constant talk about politics.
   _____ b. his knowledge of current issues.
   _____ c. his extensive reading of newspapers and magazines on these issues.
   _____ d. his assistance to a political party.
   _____ e. his frequent explanations clarifying current issues.
   _____ f. his frequent attempts to persuade and convince his classmates to work for his cause.

2. The pupil demonstrates a strong sense of self-worth as measured by

   _____ a. attempting to solve his own problems and seeking assistance only when necessary.
   _____ b. always looking for someone who would tell him how to solve his problems.
   _____ c. accepting personal criticism without becoming defensive.
   _____ d. expressing his own feelings, thoughts and reactions freely and with confidence in a group setting.
   _____ e. entering into new friendships and relationships readily.
   _____ f. putting on a show to impress people.
   _____ g. establishing his own personal standards of achievement and behavior.
   _____ h. accepting other people's values with tact and respect when they differ from his own.
   _____ i. writing a description of himself which is positive, depicting his strengths and weaknesses.
   _____ j. scoring high on the Berger Scale of *Acceptance of Self and Others.*

3. The pupil demonstrates an appreciation of the works of Matisse as measured by

_____ a. his knowledge of Matisse.
_____ b. collecting prints.
_____ c. attempting to simulate the artist's style.
_____ d. spending leisure time at the art museum when Matisse's paintings and sculptures are displayed.
_____ e. writing about the artist and his work, and describing the personal meaning it has for him.
_____ f. sharing his knowledge and appreciation with his classmates.

4. The pupil demonstrates an interest in science as measured by

_____ a. reading science magazines, books and articles in the daily newspapers.
_____ b. reporting on a science topic when given a choice of topics.
_____ c. joining science clubs.
_____ d. entering science fairs.
_____ e. spending his allowance on science equipment and books.
_____ f. borrowing numerous science books from the library.
_____ g. signing up for after-school science activities and projects.
_____ h. volunteering to assist the teacher in setting up materials for classroom use.
_____ i. volunteering to work in hospitals and health centers.

5. The pupil demonstrates that he values his family as measured by

_____ a. speaking positively about his parents and siblings.
_____ b. relating family experiences and excursions.
_____ c. writing stories and poems about members of the family focusing on their positive attributes and strengths.
_____ d. introducing parents with pride when they visit the school.

Feedback: In item 1, all of the _behaviors_ listed contribute to the measurement of the pupil's interest in the current political scene. In item 2, in dealing with an operational definition of a strong sense of self-worth, behaviors a, c, d, e, g, and h would all serve as behavioral indicators of the presence of a strong sense of self-worth, and products i and j would serve to further substantiate this. Behaviors b and f are indicative of a weak self-image. The pupil who constantly relies on others to assist him in solving problems and the pupil who needs to put on a show to impress need our help. In item 3, behaviors a, b, c, d and f and product e all serve to measure the pupil's appreciation of the works of Matisse. In item 4, an interest in science can readily be measured by behaviors a through i. In item 5, valuing the family may be measured by behaviors a, b and d and products c.

In sum, in constructing affective objectives, we will experience no difficulty if we focus on the identification of behaviors which indicate that these less tangible but critical objectives are taking place and combine these with pupil products such as written accounts, artful expressions and verbalizations.

From our experiences we are no doubt a bit cautious and skeptical as to completely accepting verbalizations, knowing that our older pupils have learned "to play the game" and give the required responses. However, our continuous observations will over a period of time clearly enable us to determine what is real and what is "for the teacher's benefit."

In constructing affective objectives and identifying behavioral indicators to measure these objectives, when difficulty arises, a strategy devised by Dr. James Popham, Dr. Eva Baker and others[1], focusing on the "attribute possessor" and "attribute nonpossessor" is very useful. What they recommend is a four-step strategy for identifying affective objectives.

We begin by clearly identifying the specific affective trait or attribute which we wish to promote and imagine an individual who possesses this trait. This imaginary individual is our "attribute possessor."

We then proceed to step 2 and now imagine an individual who does not possess this trait or is negative about it. This second individual is our "attribute nonpossessor." For example, we might be attempting to promote enjoyment in science. Our "attribute possessor" would be an imaginary individual who enjoys science; our "attribute nonpossessor" might be one who either displays no enjoyment in science or hates science.

Our third step is now to identify observable situations, natural or contrived, in which these two imagined individuals, the "attribute possessor" and the "attribute nonpossessor" should behave differently. At this point we may generate a variety of such situations, imagining how the individuals would react and determining the measureability of these reactions.

The fourth and final step in identifying our affective objectives is to compare our alternative situations and select the one which is most likely to produce the desired differences and can be readily implemented.

1. James Popham, Eva Baker, *et. al.*, *Identifying Affective Objectives*, Englewood Cliffs, Prentice Hall, Inc., 1973.

This strategy is effective and serves to provide us with the essential behavioral indicators. In brief, when we have difficulty in identifying pupils who possess a specific positive affective trait, we can readily use this "back-door" approach by focusing on the behaviors of pupils who do not possess this trait or are negative about it. Whatever "door" we use, we achieve our purpose—to provide operational definitions of affective objectives, be they behavioral indicators or products—so that we can move ahead with the affective education of the individual.

Summary

In this chapter we have worked on attaining the initial skills in writing affective objectives. We are now able to:

- differentiate between an affective goal and an affective objective.
- identify behaviors.
- classify behaviors as either overt or covert.
- identify behaviors which are highly affective, highly cognitive and highly psychomotor.
- write objectives in operational terms by selecting behavioral indicators and/or products which serve the dual purposes of identifying that affective behavior is occurring and can be measured by some practical means.

In our next chapter, we will focus in detail on performance objectives in the affective domain, measurement, mastery levels, and methods and means for affective assessment.

7 Completing the Construction of Affective Objectives

Performance Objectives

One of the outstanding "words of the decade" has been performance. The context has been in terms of objectives. In the early years of behavioral objectives, educators were generally satisfied with the term "behavioral" objective. This denoted that as a result of a series of instructional activities, the pupil's behavior changed in some positive, constructive manner. If at the "before-instruction" stage he did not speak in complete sentences and now he does so, a behavioral change is evident. If in the math classroom, he can now solve eight out of ten quadratic equations, a behavioral change is evident. If in the science classroom, he can now state Newton's third law of motion, this constitutes a behavioral change.

However, those of us who were using these behavioral objectives all too soon discovered that, in too many cases, these behavioral changes were merely verbalizations or rote procedures. Pupils were meeting the behavioral requirements; they could "solve" quadratic equations with little or no understanding of what they were doing or why they were doing it. They could rattle off a series of words which constituted Newton's third law of motion, but had no understanding of the law and its significance or practical application. What was happening was simply that behavioral change was becoming synonymous with *verbal* change, not with growth in understanding or *ability to apply* what was learned on a practical level. The critics in this case emerged from those who had favored behavioral objectives and were confronted with this glaring weakness—not that this weakness was new. The verbal game had always been played, but one of the key thrusts and major purposes of constructing behavioral objectives was to promote "real" behavioral change. Was one game merely being substituted for another, yielding the same results— ersatz verbalization? The answer emerged with the term *performance.*

If the pupil "really understood" Newton's third law of motion, he should be able to *demonstrate* this understanding by *applying* the law to actual situations. If the pupil really mastered the basic skills of computation, he should be able to *use* them in problem-solving situations, knowing precisely when to add, multiply, subtract and divide. In essence, he should be able to *perform.* In the basic skills areas and in the cognitive areas, *performance* was definitely a more valid instrument for measuring behavioral change. Verbalization was a problem, for we had no way of knowing whether the pupil understood the words he was using or had merely memorized them. Memory no doubt had its place, but it had to be coupled with understanding. Therefore a change was instituted: *wherever possible,* teachers were urged to state their objectives in *performance terms*—have the pupil *use* the skill or knowledge, *act upon it and apply it.*

In the affective domain, performance was equally essential. Our pupils can readily tell us that they value honesty, that they should treat each other with respect and dignity, that human beings should share, cooperate, assist each other, and care about other's feelings and concerns, *but unless they act upon these values and put them into practice, they remain worthless verbalizations.* We are back to that old cliche, "Never mind what he says, what does he do?" "Actions speak louder than words!" What we were searching for were *action objectives!*

To make this transition on a practical level does require time and readjustment. We do not expect the change to occur overnight. It takes continuous effort and time to communicate to our pupils that words are not sufficient. For us, in our role as teachers, we need to revise instructional activities so that we go beyond the verbalization stage to the action or performance stage. In structuring our instruction, we continuously are required to ask ourselves how the pupil can *apply* this knowledge or skill—cognitive, affective or psychomotor— to demonstrate that he "really understands" it or "really values" it. *Application is the key word.* You and I can read a manual on how to drive a car, but the true test is not a composition on "How I Drive a Car," but driving that car correctly and safely.

In the affective domain, you and I may have a very warm, friendly and understanding discussion on how we value the individuality of people, but again the true test is in how we treat others—*how we behave, perform and interact,* not only verbally but on a more complex level encompassing all of the messages we convey, how we structure situations and allow others to behave as unique individuals. A glance, a body movement all too often betray a verbal statement.

In sum, constructing behavioral objectives so that performance is incorporated whenever and wherever it is realistically possible is the best course of action.

In working paper #5, we have achieved this to a large extent—our behavioral indicators were observations of actions; our products, however, were in many cases forms of verbalizations. Each reinforced the other. Again, let us maintain a realistic perspective—we cannot totally discard verbalization, but we can work toward greater emphasis on performance.

We must exercise care in our interpretation of *verbalization.* There are times when verbalization does denote a performance. If we feel strongly about a political issue and write a letter to an editor or make a speech to a group, the verbalization in this context is a performance. Therefore, we are distinguishing between *mere verbal expression* and verbal expression which is an authentic performance. Here our professional judgment and knowledge of our pupils serves us to distinguish which is which!

In working paper #6, *Performance Objectives in the Affective Domain,* you will develop skill in identifying affective performance so that, in the long run, mere verbalizations may be translated into actions.

Working Paper #6
Performance Objectives in the Affective Domain

Objective: Given a semantic guide, you will be able to identify those affective objectives which describe a performance and are written in performance terms.

Semantic Guide:

A performance—*an observable action or set of actions* which clearly demonstrate that the pupil is *applying* skills, knowledge (concepts, generalizations and data) values, interests and appreciations to actual situations.

Criterion Questions

The key questions which serve to identify an objective which is stated in performance terms are:

1. How does the pupil who attains this objective *perform*?

2. Does the objective, as stated, elicit only verbalization or does it require the pupil to *demonstrate the application of* skills, knowledge or affect by performing, behaving and acting in some way in response to a given situation?

3. Does the objective as stated elicit only verbalization, simply because verbalization is the required and sufficient behavioral response?

If in answering these questions we find that the pupil is responding by applying skills and knowledge values to a situation and *acting on these,* the objective is stated in performance terms. However, in the case where verbalization is all that is required, the objective is stated in *behavioral terms*. To eliminate confusion, it is best to limit performance to pupil actions which clearly demonstrate application and *preclude verbalizations*. Our purpose is to minimize the acceptance of "telling or written behavior" that "snows us" and to emphasize real, authentic performance. In response to question 3, the answer may be yes, the objective calls for verbalization and at this stage of affective growth verbalization is sufficient. This in no way diminishes the objective. However, we classify it as a *behavioral objective* rather than a performance objective.

Directions: Examine the following affective objectives and place a *P* in front of each one which designates that performance is taking place and a *V* in front of each one which designates a verbalization.

_____ 1. The pupil demonstrates his value of trusting others by writing a composition on "Why Trust Among People is Important."

_____ 2. The pupil demonstrates his value of trusting others by enthusiastically going on a "Trust Walk" with a classmate in which he is blindfolded and led around the school yard.

_____ 3. The pupil demonstrates his value of trusting others by lending his one set of notes to a classmate so that he may study for a test.

_____ 4. The pupil demonstrates his value of trusting others by lending a classmate money for lunch.

_____ 5. The pupil demonstrates his strong belief in racial equality by treating all of his classmates with equal respect and dignity.

_____ 6. The pupil demonstrates his strong belief in racial equality by joining clubs or local organizations which promote racial equality.

_____ 7. The pupil demonstrates his strong belief in racial equality by attending a rally for racial equality.

_____ 8. The pupil demonstrates his strong belief in racial equality by visiting a ghetto to survey the living conditions.

_____ 9. The pupil demonstrates an interest in health care and research by collecting money for lung cancer, leukemia and heart disease research.

_____ 10. The pupil demonstrates an interest in health care and research by working as a volunteer in a local hospital after school, on weekends or during vacations.

Feedback: Items 2, 3, 4, 5, 6, 7, 8, 9 and 10 were affective objectives written in performance terms. All were _actions_ translating values, beliefs and interests. Item 1, in keeping with our definitions, was a verbalization. Here the pupil used written expression to demonstrate his value of trusting others.

In sum, considering the state of education with its excessive reliance on verbalization, it is time we attempted to shift the emphasis to increased use of performance.

Direct and Indirect Measurement

We can readily see how measurement in the affective domain may become a problem if we persist in attempting to put square pegs into round holes. One of the major purposes in constructing objectives is to focus on the measurement of their attainment. We want to be able to communicate clearly what the pupil will be able to do as a result of a series of instructional activities and how we will "know" with some degree of certainty that he can do so.

To spend countless hours in constructing the stem of the objective, stating what the pupil will be able to do without specifying how this will be measured is an exercise in futility. It is comparable to the efforts of those dedicated educators who rediscovered the process of diagnosis, diagnosed the pupil's weaknesses and entry behaviors, but found themselves at a loss when they were unable to "fill" the diverse instructional prescription to realistically meet individual needs. They were caught up in the dilemma of Diagnosis—So What?

When we deal with measurability in the skill areas of the three R's or in the rote recall of data, we have few problems, if any. The pupil counts, adds, multiplies, reads, spells, writes, punctuates, selects the correct answer, and states the specific data. The measurement is observable and direct.

However, when we are intent on promoting affective growth, when we are dealing with the exploration of feelings, beliefs, attitudes, interests, appreciations, values and the development of a strong and positive self-concept, measurement is not readily observable or direct. On the contrary, we are searching for behavioral indicators, for products which will in some way, with some degree of certainty, tell us that these affective objectives are being attained. In sum, in the affective domain as well as in the higher levels of the cognitive domain, we rely on *indirect methods of measurement,* we rely on placing pupils in situations where they will perform in a specific manner, we rely on products and oral, written and artistic expressions, to substantiate affective behavioral change.

For example, when pupils are asked to explore how they feel, how they react to a specific poem, play or musical recording and to compare the "feelings" reactions of the group, we, as teachers, have no *direct* way of knowing what these feelings are or if our pupils are comparing these feelings. Only when our pupils express them orally or list them in written form do we "know" this has occurred. The statement of feelings and the lists of similarities and differences of "feelings" reactions are the behaviors and products which indicate that our pupils have explored their feelings and have compared the feelings of the individuals in the group.

In the use of any of the process skills: observation, comparison, classification, analysis, critical thinking, creative thinking, etc., when applied to either of the two domains, measurement is always indirect and dependent on a product or a behavioral indicator. This is not to say that affective and highly cognitive behaviors defy measurement. They are measurable. Our measurements, however, are indirect in all of these cases. As long as we focus on indirect means, our search will not be difficult. As long as we are truly committed to the development of the humanizing components of the individual and reinforce our words with our efforts, we will be motivated to search and identify indirect means to measure affective growth.

In working paper #7, *Measurability in the Affective Domain,* we will develop skill in identifying behaviors which are directly measurable and those which require indirect means such as behavioral indicators or products.

Working Paper #7
Measurability in the Affective Domain

Objective: Given a semantic guide, you will be able to identify those behaviors which are directly measurable and those which are indirectly measurable, requiring behavioral indicators or products to demonstrate that these objectives are being attained.

Semantic Guide:

Directly Measurable—We label a behavior as directly measurable when we are able to *observe* it and are able to establish specific criteria with which to measure it.

Indirectly Measurable—We label a behavior indirectly measurable when we cannot observe it directly. It is one that can be measured by *behavioral indicators* or *pupil products.* For example, if a pupil is very interested in a particular subject, the teacher may observe this indirectly by specific behavioral indicators such as: the pupil reads many books on the subject; he asks many questions; he returns after school and requests further information and resources. Or the teacher may discover the pupil's interest from a *product* such as *an essay or an article the pupil has written.*

Directions: Examine the following objectives. Categorize each objective by placing a *DM* in front of each one which is directly measurable, an *IDM* in front of each which is indirectly measurable, a *Pr* in front of each *component of the objective* where a product is used as an indirect measurement and a *BI* where a behavioral indicator is used as an indirect measurement.

1. The pupil demonstrates his ability to be self-directive by

   _____ a. choosing freely from a variety of projects the one in which he is most interested.

   _____ b. submitting his project plans on paper in a step-by-step sequence.

   _____ c. submitting a list of materials and resources he will need for the project.

   _____ d. submitting his completed project when it is due.

   _____ e. evaluating his project utilizing his own criteria by listing its strengths and weaknesses.

2. The pupil demonstrates his ability to make decisions by

_____ a. identifying his problem in written form.

_____ b. exploring his feelings in regard to the problem by listing them.

_____ c. listing the options he perceives as being available to him in solving his problem.

_____ d. evaluating the options by listing them and compiling the pros and cons of each.

_____ e. ordering the options in terms of his most important values.

_____ f. reaching a decision by selecting a course of action and taking that course of action.

3. The pupil demonstrates his belief in and valuing of the work ethic by

_____ writing an essay describing three successful people whom he admires and describing how their success in each case can be attributed to their application of the work ethic.

4. The pupil demonstrates his interest in and appreciation of folk music by

_____ a. joining a folk music group.

_____ b. collecting records of folk music.

_____ c. doing odd jobs to earn money to attend folk music concerts.

_____ d. reading books, newspaper and magazine accounts on the lives of famous folk singers.

_____ e. enthusiastically discussing folk music and folk musicians whenever an opportunity arises.

5. The pupil demonstrates his skill in playing folk music by

_____ bringing his guitar to class and playing a variety of folk songs for his classmates.

Feedback: The only objective of the five given which was directly measurable was number 5. Here the pupil demonstrated his skill in playing folk music by doing so. Objective 5 as stated was a skill objective. Objectives 1, 2, 3 and 4 were affective objectives dealing with self-directive behavior, decision-making, belief in and valuing the work ethic and demonstrating an interest in and appreciation of folk music. All of these objectives were not directly measurable, but indirectly measurable, IDM. The components of each of the objectives were either products or behavioral indicators.

In objective 1, component a, choosing freely, served as a behavioral indicator; b, c, d, e were all products, namely the project plans, the list of materials, the completed project and the written self-evaluation of the project.

In objective 2, components a, b, c, d, and e were all products, written statements or lists indicating that the decision-making process was taking place. Component f, selecting a course of action and taking it, was a behavioral indicator that the decision-making process was completed and being acted upon.

In objective 3, the pupil demonstrated his belief in and valuing of the work ethic by producing a product or an essay.

In objective 4, the pupil demonstrated his interest in and appreciation of folk music by behavioral indicators—joining a club, collecting records, attending concerts, reading and discussing folk music enthusiastically.

In sum, when we are dealing with affective objectives, our measurements are indirect and include either products or behavioral indicators or a mixture of both. Measurement in the affective domain requires greater effort than in the "basic" skill areas and is not simple—but then neither are people!

Discussion Paper #8
Affective Mastery Levels?

The current thrust on establishing mastery levels in the skill areas and in the conventional content areas is readily understandable. For years, in fact for decades, the critical need to teach-them-all-to-read-and-to-compute has been dramatically expressed. Now, more than ever before, educators, parents and the public at large are greatly concerned with the lack of mastery in the skill areas. Published test results and comparative data demonstrating a decline in literacy have served to intensify efforts to focus on these skills.

In constructing objectives, educators feeling these pressures are not only specifying how these objectives will be measured, but are spelling out mastery levels, namely the minimal level of acceptable performance required of the pupils. For example, a statement such as: the pupil will be able to solve 8 out of 10 quadratic equations clearly denotes that in order to "pass" the pupil must give 8 out of 10 correct responses in solving quadratic equations. In citing mastery levels for computational skills such as addition, subtraction, multiplication and division, 100 percent mastery is required.

School systems involved in the Planning Programming, Budgeting, Evaluation System have prefaced each objective with: 80 percent of the pupils will be able to . . . . Whether 80 percent of their pupils will or will not is not the key issue, the key issue is that mastery levels in these skill areas have not been enforced, that pupils have been "promoted" automatically and that we are now confronted with the snowball effect. Unfortunate as this situation is, it must be dealt with on a realistic level. The first step, obviously, is to establish realistic mastery levels and to adhere to them. At this point, I will make no attempt to deal with the type of differentiated instruction required to meet the needs of diverse pupil populations. The point is that in these areas, mastery levels are essential.

Since our focus is on the affective domain, the question of mastery levels is again raised. Should we specify mastery levels in the affective domain? Should we be stating that: 80 percent of our pupils will demonstrate self-directive behavior or are demonstrating a more positive self-concept? Ideally, yes; realistically, no! Affective education is definitely in its early stage of growth. The climate and soil essential for its growth is one of openness, of warmth, of freedom to explore, of providing for subjective expression. To impose mastery levels in the affective domain would be totally detrimental to its major purposes. We are dealing with the subjective realm; we are attempting to promote the emergence of the inner self, the person, the personality, the sensitive core of the human being—his humanism.

In this domain, we are concerned with qualities such as compassion, fulfillment, caring, affection and understanding oneself; our focus is not on objectivity but on subjectivity. Therefore to attempt to be objective about the subjective, to establish mastery levels, minimal levels of acceptable "becoming," to mark or grade affective behavior, to expect an individual to earn a perfect grade on the test of humanity, or to expect him to "complete" a strong and positive self-image would be utterly ridiculous. We are dealing with the development of humaneness and humanness. We are dealing with a self-image which always remains to some extent incomplete, with a process of "becoming" that is continuous throughout our lives. To institute mastery levels and a grading system with its accompanying negative effects—competitiveness between pupils, comparisons of pupils, pressure to excel, and the stigma of failure would in essence result in dehumanizing humanism.

The age-old problem rears its ugly head. Are grades essential? Must measurement be conducted on a grading scale or are there other more positive methods of assessing mastery and behavioral change which do not destroy one-half of the learner at the expense of the other half? Would parent, pupils and teachers be content with "Yes, you have mastered X, Y and Z skills," or "No, you have not *yet* mastered X, Y and Z skills." There is little doubt that as educators we need to reassess the grading system, but let us return to the issue at hand, the measurement of affective behavior.

As a humanistic teacher, I am very concerned with my pupil's self-image, with his feelings, interests, appreciations and values. I certainly want to be able to "know" if my instructional program is promoting these significant traits. For this pupose, I have no need for either letters of the alphabet nor for numerals. There are certainly more positive and constructive ways to measure and assess. Can I simply assess his behaviors by observing him and keeping a descriptive account of the changes I observe? Does not a written account or a checklist of affective objectives and behaviors provide me with a more precise operational profile of my pupils than a grade? The obvious answer is yes. We can use descriptive assessment.

But another major question arises. If these are significant traits—and they are—should we rely *solely* on observational techniques or are there other means to measure the growth of these traits and provide greater validity to our results? The answer again is yes, we can supplement our observations with affective "tests" and with the assessment of pupil products.

In sum, up to this point, we have stressed the dire and realistic need to establish mastery levels in the skills and knowledge areas. Lest I be misunderstood, these mastery levels need not be accompanied by grades; they may be checked off in terms of "mastered" or "yet-to-be-mastered." In the affective domain, mastery levels are inappropriate and unrealistic. In their place, descriptive assessment is one answer. We are now ready to explore other means of affective measurement.

Instruments For Affective Assessment

Obviously we do not plan to "test" for affective growth in the conventional sense. Were we to do so, the likelihood of stifling this growth and reducing affective learning would be great. However, we are concerned with affective growth and its measurement. The task in this case is not simple. We are not measuring for the mastery of rote skills nor for the recall of data. The means and instruments to measure self-concept and its components, beliefs, interests, appreciations, values are highly susceptible to human weakness and error. In the affective domain, the instruments available to us consist of a variety of inventories, questionnaires, and scales dealing with one's self-concept, one's beliefs about diverse issues, one's attitudes, values, personality, motivation, and feelings of sympathy and empathy, to name but a few. These instruments are essentially self-report devices and require the pupil to respond to a series of very direct questions.

In using these devices, the pupil clearly understands the intent of the questions; no camouflage exists. The pupil may respond honestly or may give what he perceives to be the desired response. Since pupils have been conditioned to give the "right answer," we cannot realistically underestimate the tendency to fake. In using these measures, our only recourse to minimize the faking response is to impress our pupils with the value of leveling, honest replies, pointing out that there is no one right answer, but only an answer that is and feels right for each individual. After a short period of time, pupils do respond sincerely and honestly to these inventories and questionnaires. They report freely on their feelings, beliefs, opinions, interests and appreciations. Their investment is great; the self wins out!

Specifically for educational purposes, self-report devices such as the various self-concept inventories, the attitude toward school and education inventories, the interest assessment scales, the impulsivity scales such as *What I Like To Do,* and the reading attitude inventories such as *How I Feel* which assesses primary pupils' attitude toward school and reading should be of vital interest to us.

Among the most useful for the classroom teacher have been those focusing on the pupil's self-concept. For example, the self-report instrument *About Me,* available from James Parker, Department of Education, Georgia Southern College, Slatesboro, Georgia, is a very practical instrument. It assesses five areas of self-concept; namely, the self, the self in relation to others, the self as achieving, the self in school and the physical self. There are six items for each of the five areas.

Each of the 30 items consists of a positive and a negative statement on opposite ends of a continuum. The pupil rates himself along a five-point scale between the two statements. The following are sample items taken from the instrument.

1   2   3   4   5

I'm good in school work   I'm not good in school work

I'm popular   I'm not too popular

I'm not tall enough   I'm tall enough
I'm proud of me   I'm not proud of me

About Me was constructed for use in a dissertation study. It is appropriate for students in grades four through six. Individual or group administration is possible. No rigorous normative or statistical data are available. Scores are derived by summing the numerical values of individual items. High scores indicate a negative self-concept; low scores a positive self concept.

Another example of a direct self-report device focusing on the self-concept is the *Self Appraisal Inventory*, available for the primary, intermediate and secondary levels from the Instructional Objectives Exchange, P.O. Box 24095, Los Angeles, California 90024, which was established in 1968 by the UCLA Center for the Study of Evaluation. This instrument provides a general profile of the pupil's self-concept as well as subscale scores dealing with data along the following dimensions (1) family, the pupil's self-concept based on family interactions, (2) peer relations, the pupil's self-concept based on peer interactions, (3) scholastic achievement, the pupil's self-concept resulting from success or failures in scholastic endeavors, and (4) general, a comprehensive estimate of how the self is viewed. This inventory can be used in part or in whole, based on your specific objectives. The directions are clear-cut; the scoring is uncomplicated. It is designed to be used on both a pre- and post- instructional basis. The instructional period should be lengthy. The instrument could be used at the beginning of the school year as a pre-test and at the close of the year as a post-test. Recommendations for flexible use of the instrument are spelled out in detail.

The following are sample items taken from the *Self Appraisal Inventory*, primary level. Pupils respond with a "yes" or "no" and scores are obtained by counting one point for each *positive* response, *a favorable view of the self.*

1. Are you easy to like?
2. Do you often get in trouble at home?
3. Can you give a good talk in front of your class?
4. Do you wish you were younger?
5. Do you usually let other children have their way?
6. Are you an important person to your family?

These direct self-report devices are excellent tools in providing the teacher with an affective profile of the growth of individual pupils as in the case of *About Me* or in providing a general picture of the progress of a class over a substantial period of time such as in the use of the *Self Appraisal Inventory,* which is designed to secure anonymous responses and to evaluate a group.

Teachers have found that their exposure to these instruments have motivated them to construct their own brief inventories for classroom use and have given them greater insights into their pupil's behavioral patterns.

In using any of these instruments, care must be exercised in making certain that the instrument or the parts being used clearly reflect the affective objectives of instruction. All too often, we have made the assumptions that we are clearly assessing for what we have taught. Before using any instrument, compare its objectives with your own. In the cognitive domain, research clearly indicates that although teachers believe they are testing for what they have taught, this is by no means the case. However, if we are equipped with specific objectives, we should have little difficulty in matching the "test" items or the assessment instrument with these objectives. *Making the match* is of vital importance. In working paper #9 which follows, you will test your skill in matching affective objectives with affective measures of assessment.

Working Paper #9
Matching Affective Objectives With
Affective "Tests" and Indicators

Objective: You will be able to identify and apply the essential relationship between specified affective objectives and the selection and/or construction of test items, performance tasks, self-reporting devices, direct observations and pupil products to measure the attainment of these objectives.

Criterion Questions: The following questions will assist you in making the match between the objective and the means of measuring its attainment:

1. What specifically do you want the pupil to be able to do or demonstrate?

2. Does your method of measurement serve to assess this behavior as validly as is *realistically possible?*

Directions:

I. Take each of the following objectives and *make the match* from the many alternatives given.

1. The pupil freely expresses his feelings about a member of his family whom he greatly admires as measured by

    _____ a. describing the individual's strong points and explaining why he values these attributes.

    _____ b. writing a short essay on the importance of the family and its effects on modern society.

    _____ c. describing each member of his or her family and their roles.

2. Given a story, the pupil gives his own interpretation of the story expressing its relevance to him as measured by

    _____ a. a description of each of the characters in the story.

    _____ b. an outline of the plot of the story.

    _____ c. an outline of the sequence of events in the story.

    _____ d. a description of the feelings and thoughts he experienced as he read the story and the values it had for him.

3. Given an issue such as gun control, the pupil takes a stand on the issue as measured by

    _____ a. listing the pros and cons of the issue.

    _____ b. expressing his opinion and substantiating it with data.

    _____ c. describing the effects of the lack of gun control on city dwellers.

II. Column A contains a list of affective objectives. Column B contains instruments and means to measure these objectives. How would you match them? Some of the items in Column B may be used more than once. The pupil will

The pupil will	As measured by
_____ 1. increase his knowledge of interpersonal relationships	A. Gordon's "How I See Myself" Scale
_____ 2. value freedom	B. Teacher observation
_____ 3. appreciate mathematics	C. Reading books
_____ 4. improve his self-concept	D. Math Attitude Scale
_____ 5. listen to and accept others' viewpoints	E. Reading more difficult books
_____ 6. demonstrate increased confidence in his reading ability.	F. Improve attendance record
_____ 7. assume greater responsibility for his work and behavior	G. Student and Teacher Global Social Climate Scale
	H. Greater effort and completion of tasks on time
	I. The Academic Freedom Survey

_____ 8. interact more freely
with his classmates

Feedback: In item 1, dealing with the pupil's free expression in regard to a member of his family whom he greatly admires, the means of measurement is a—by describing the individual's strong points and explaining why he values these attributes.

In item 2, dealing with the pupil's interpretation of a story expressing its relevance to him, component d. is the means of measurement. In this case, we do not deal with the cognitive data—with the facts per se—but with the pupil's own reactions to the facts.

In item 3, we can measure the pupil's taking a stand on an issue by actually observing him doing so; component b is our means of measurement.

In matching columns A and B, the task was relatively easy. The results are as follows:

C	1. increase his knowledge of interpersonal relationships
I	2. value freedom
D	3. appreciate mathematics
A	4. improve his self-concept
B	5. listen to and accept others' viewpoints
E	6. demonstrate increased confidence in his reading ability
H	7. assume greater responsibility for his work and behavior
B	8. interact more freely with his classmates.

As you have probably discovered in completing this working paper, making the match between the objective and its means of measurement is a relatively simple task. It is both logical and right that we do assess and measure, at a realistic and constructive level, for what we have taught.

Summary

We have now acquired all of the basic skills which constitute the construction of objectives in the affective domain. In Chapters 6 and 7 your experiences with working and discussion papers 1 through 9 specifically enabled you to:

- Differentiate between an affective goal and a specific affective objective

- Identify a behavior as an action, interaction or reaction on the part of the individual
- Differentiate between an overt observable behavior and one that is covert or hidden or not always readily observable
- Identify, for practical purposes, behaviors which are highly cognitive, highly affective and highly psychomotor
- Operationalize affective behaviors by combining general terms with highly specific ones
- Identify performance objectives in the affective domain
- Identify behaviors which are directly measurable and those which require indirect means such as behavioral indicators or products
- Pinpoint the need for mastery levels in the skills and cognitive areas, but not in the affective domain
- Identify various instruments, self-report devices, questionnaires scales and inventories to assess affective growth
- Make the match between affective objectives and affective means of measurement and assessment

Equipped with these skills, we are now ready to proceed to the next step of our blueprint, that of integrating the cognitive and affective components into a balanced affective and cognitive curriculum.

A Curriculum for the Seventies and Eighties: The Affective and Cognitive Curriculum

The Task Ahead

Equipped with a rationale for "getting-down-to-basics", an operational definition of the key components of the self-concept, process skills and strategies which are readily applicable to both cognitive and affective learning, and the essential know-how in constructing affective objectives, we are prepared to take another major step outlined in our blueprint for education in Chapter 1—that of modifying our school's existing curriculum to produce a balanced and integrated affective and cognitive curriculum that is both valid and viable for the seventies and the eighties. The mere thought of attempting to do so may at first appear to be overwhelming, but in practice this is not the case.

Constructing Affective and Cognitive Learning Units

We begin by following a sequential plan which is outlined in the following pages and enables us to construct learning units. The unit approach enables us to function within our existing framework and simultaneously modify our curriculum so that the transition is gradual. These units are constructed and classroom tested, needed modifications are made, and the units are then made available to all staff members. The total process is a gradual one characterized by continuous assistance, support and feedback. There is no thrust on "starting tomorrow." Teachers work at their own pace, individually or in small groups and interact freely with principals, supervisors and consultants.

The affective-cognitive learning unit which is constructed is a modification of the Behavioral Outcomes Learning Units which were initially created by cadres of teachers of the Norwalk Public Schools in Connecticut under a grant from the Fund for the Advancement of Education, an agency of the Ford Foundation. The Norwalk School System focused on cognitive learning. As numerous other school systems began to utilize this model and the affective aspects became more and more apparent, these staffs saw the need to incorporate the affective components and to establish a balance. An affective-cognitive Behavioral Outcomes model of a learning unit emerged.

This affective-cognitive learning unit clearly depicts a different and balanced philosophy of education. Education is viewed and practiced as a *thinking-valuing process*. The focus of the unit is on the pupil as an active interactor operating on four levels: the knowledge level, which deals with concepts, generalizations and factual data; the skills level which encompasses tool skills such as the 3 Rs and specific skills such as the use of a microscope, protractor, slide rule, etc.; the values levels, which deals with feelings, emotions, belief systems and values, and the most significant level, the action level, which focuses on the *application* of knowledge, skills and values to situations requiring actual behavior and performance.

The Essential Steps in Constructing Effective Learning Units

Given this framework, we will examine the basic sequential steps in constructing the learning unit.

Step 1—Preparing a Preface

We prepare a preface by constructing an outline describing in broad and general terms the overall objectives of the unit. We identify the key concepts, fundamental skills, values or value-centered issues and the kinds of actions or performances pupils will engage in to demonstrate that some behavioral change has taken place.

To illustrate we will use a preface page from an affective-cognitive unit fusing social studies and science, "Why Bother About Soil Conservation?"

Preface

The purposes of this unit are to enable the pupil to:

1. Acquire some basic knowledge of man's dependence on the soil, focusing on his use and abuse of soil, forests and grasslands.

2. Demonstrate that the misuse of one natural resource directly affects other resources.

3. Explain how natural phenomena and man's misuse of land have resulted in great losses of topsoil and natural vegetation.

4. Explain how soil scientists have helped farmers and landowners take better care of the soil.

5. Construct models and demonstrate how terracing and contour plowing have prevented the erosion of important topsoil.

6. Demonstrate valuing conservation practices by taking some constructive action and sustaining these efforts throughout the school year.

7. Relate the problems of soil conservation to his own community by identifying areas where misuse is taking place and identifying how these practices affect life in his community.

8. Devise action-projects which serve to *build an awareness in the school and the community* of these conservation needs by initiating concrete action. Possible projects include:
    a. Visits to the local Health Department and Conservation Commission to discover what kinds of constructive actions are being taken.
    b. Interviews with people who work with natural resources, such as farmers, lumbermen, miners, fishermen, etc.
    c. Interviews with local representatives of business and industry to determine their views and practices in this area.
    d. Exploration of the school grounds and community to identify constructive and destructive practices.
    e. Research on what other communities have done in this area.
    f. Letters to local newspapers and local officials on the value of sound conservation practices.
    g. Creation of posters, slogans, poems, songs, slide shows, videotapes, models to be shown in schools and local banks to foster community awareness and action.
    h. Organizing cleanup and assistance campaigns.

9. Apply the fundamental skills of reading, composition and research as well as the creative skills in completing his project.

10. Compile a list of books, articles and pamphlets which he views as relevant to the issue and would recommend to others.

11. Assess his project and those of his classmates to determine whether the "study" of this unit had any real effects on all involved.

This preface serves other specific and practical purposes. Since these units, following classroom testing and modification, are made available to all teachers at a specific grade level, a rapid perusal of the preface enables the teacher to decide whether the unit is suitable for his or her class or for small groups of pupils within the class who have demonstrated an interest in the unit's issues.

Some teachers have found that they need not use the unit in its entirety. Parts of the unit are used and tailored to specific groups of pupils. Teachers have found it helpful to attach their modifications to the unit. In many cases, pupils raised additional issues and suggested community-oriented activities. These too were noted in the unit. The result was a variety of versions of the "same" unit which incorporated both teacher and pupil inputs. In other cases where community members were active participants, further inputs were included. It was rare that a unit following classroom implementation did not undergo some significant modification.

Step 2—Constructing a Content Outline

Having stated in broad terms what the overall objectives of our unit are, we now proceed to identify the specific content which our pupils will process cognitively and affectively to achieve these goals.

Our content outline centers on the four levels of learning. We therefore classify the content of the unit under four headings: the knowledge level, the skills level, the values level and the action level. Under knowledge we make a *sequential* list of the concepts, generalizations and factual data of the unit in the order in which the material will be presented. Under tool skills, we enumerate the general skills such as reading, writing and composition, as well as the specific tool skills such as research skills, science skills, and opportunities for creativity. Under values, we list specific attitudes, values and issues we plan to analyze and classify. Under actions, we list the behaviors and performances which demonstrate application of knowledge, skills and values to actual situations.

Following our initial draft, we review each category to check that the sequence is logical and efficient. The sequence is logical in each category if each item as listed is a precondition or entry behavior or skill for the one which follows it. The sequence is efficient if there is a minimal need to go back, review and reteach as the unit progresses.

We then review the total content outline in terms of the relevancy of the items we have incorporated. Do we have a valid rationale for each of these items? If asked by our pupils, "Why are we learning this?" can we readily respond and substantiate our curricular decision?

The content outline should be operational and sufficiently specific for *your purpose*.

As a sample let's examine the content outline of the unit, "Why Bother About Soil Conservation?"

Content Outline

I. *Knowledge Level*

Concepts

Soil (topsoil, subsoil)
Forest
Grassland
Erosion
Drought
Conservation

Generalizations

1. We are totally dependent upon our soil and land for our survival.
2. Natural phenomena have caused a loss of large quantities of topsoil and natural vegetation.
3. Man's abuse and misuse of soil, forests and grasslands has resulted in great losses of land.
4. Man can protect and restore his natural resources.

Factual Data

Definitions of:
minerals
humus
loam
terracing
contour plowing
furrows
cover crops
controlled grazing

II. *Skills Level*

A. *Tool Skills*
Reading
Writing
Composition
Measurement

B. *Specific Skills*
Research skills
Model building

III. *Values Level*

  A. *Experiences To Sensitize Pupils* (Choice of two or more)

  - Visit areas in the community to identify where abuse and and misuse of soil is taking place. Report on what you saw and how you felt. Suggest what could be done.

  - Visit local Health and/or Conservation Commissions, interview staff members and report on what is being done.

  - Interview people who work with natural resources.

  - Interview local representatives of business and industry and describe their attitudes, views and practices.

  B. *Discussion, Analysis and Decision-Making Based on Sensitizing Experiences*

  - From the data you have gathered, do you think an action program is needed to make better choices about soil and land use?

  - What kinds of attitudes did you sense in your visits and interviews?

  - What were your reactions to these experiences?

  - Are there jobs you and your classmates could do to help the community?

  - Is community awareness a problem? How can we tackle it?

  - Have we done enough up to this point? What courses of action could we take?

IV. *Action Level*

  - Research on actions of other communities

  - Letters to local newspapers and local officials

  - Creation of posters, slogans, poems, etc., to foster community awareness

  - Cleanup and assistance campaigns

  - Schoolwide contests to foster pupil awareness

  - Cooperation with community groups and organizations to promote change.

Step 3—Specifying the Pupil's Objectives At the Four Levels in Behavioral and/or Performance and Measurable Terms

Equipped with a content outline, we proceed to construct a series of specific objectives in behavioral and/or performance, and in measurable terms. Having the content outline before us as a guide, we simply state what the pupil will be able to do as a result of his interaction with this cognitive and affective content.

Let's illustrate the process by using our sample unit. We will begin by using our objectives at the knowledge level and deal with the six concepts in our outline.

Specific Behavioral Objectives— Knowledge Level—Concepts

1. The pupil will demonstrate his concept of soil by
   a. identifying a sample of soil from a variety of samples of different materials.
   b. describing briefly the key ingredients of top soil.
   c. listing at least three major uses of soil.
2. The pupil will demonstrate his concepts of forest and grassland by describing the key characteristics of each and listing at least two ways in which a forest differs from a grassland.
3. The pupil will demonstrate his conception of erosion by either drawing a picture of an area which has been eroded or by providing a description of water or wind erosion.
4. Given a variety of pictures, the pupil will demonstrate his concept of drought by correctly identifying an area affected by drought.
5. The pupil will demonstrate his conception of conservation by describing in his own words what a person who conserves natural resources does.

Specific Behavioral Objectives— Knowledge Level—Generalizations

In constructing the specific objectives in terms of the pupil's acquisition of the four generalizations in this unit, various formats are readily used. For example: "Given the generalization that _____ (insert any one of the four), the pupil will be able to substantiate this principle by citing at least three examples in which it applies." Another format we may use is this: "Given the generalization that _____ (insert any one of the four) and three sample situations, the pupil will correctly identify the two situations to which the generalization is applicable." Still another format we may use is: "Given three sample situations (all of which are illustrations of X generalization), the pupil will compare the situations, identify what is common to all and elicit and state the generalization."

Specific Behavioral Objectives—
Knowledge Level—Factual Data

Here the task is at a rote level. In our content outline we required definitions of eight terms. Therefore the format for our specific objective is simply: "Given the following terms (list all) the pupil will provide a correct definition of each." For those of our pupils who have difficulty in defining terms, our objective reads: "Given a variety of pictures and illustrations and a list of the following terms _____ (insert the terms), the pupil will be able to match the correct term with the correct picture or illustration."

Specific Behavioral Objectives—Skills Level—
Tool Skills and Specific Skills

The kinds of objectives which are the easiest to construct are those dealing with the skills level. In our sample unit, using our content outline as a guide, we have identified the tool skills of reading, writing, composition and measurement as well as the specific skills of research and model building. The format for our specific objective is: "The pupil will demonstrate skill in _____ (insert the skill) as measured by _____ (insert a product)." For example, in the case of reading, the objective would read as follows: "The pupil will demonstrate skill in reading with comprehension as measured by the completeness of a written or oral summary."

Specifying Behavioral Objectives—Values Level

In specifying objectives at the values level as described in detail in Chapters 6 and 7, the task is by no means insurmountable. In our sample unit, our objective is that the pupil value conservation of natural resources. The premise upon which we operate is that, if one values something, one demonstrates this value by taking constructive action. Therefore the format we use is: "The pupil will demonstrate that he values _____ (insert the value) as measured by _____ (list the action or actions)." To cite an example: "The pupil will demonstrate that he values conservation of natural resources as measured by one or more of the following behaviors: a. writes a letter to the local newspaper urging improved conservation practices; b. organizes or participates in a community conservation plan; c. produces a slide show on the need for conservation which is disseminated to other schools and local banks to promote community awareness.

In sum, in step 3, we specify all of our objectives at the four levels of learning. We then place them into the sequence in which they will be used in the instructional plan. The sequence which has been found to be most effective consists of starting the unit on the cognitive level, proceeding to the values level, and concluding on the action level. The tool skills objectives are interdispersed throughout the unit since they are functional. In many cases, variations in sequence have taken place. For example, pupils are confronted with a problem, begin their operations at the cognitive level, move on to the affective or values level, find their data inadequate, return to the cognitive level and then proceed to the values level and finally to the action level. Teachers have found that flexible sequencing is readily attained once they are equipped with a listing of their objectives. The objectives serve as the base for the construction of the learning unit.

Step 4—Selecting The Process Skills To Be Used In Attaining The Objectives

In step 4, equipped with our sequential list of objectives, we as the designers of the curriculum, make the key decision—that of selecting the process skills which will be *used by the pupils* in attaining these objectives. We must keep in mind that what is central to this approach is *processing* and that the common threads running through this affective-cognitive curriculum are the process skills. The expanded Behavioral Outcomes Approach which we are utilizing is a process-centered, affective and cognitive instructional system. Its major thrust is on the development of the *pupil's processing skills* which are to be applied to *both cognitive and affective data.* The outcomes of this approach are three-fold: pupils develop competency in the process skills, acquire cognitive structures (concepts, generalizations, data) and acquire affective structures (knowledge of self and one's values).

Therefore before we can move ahead to outline our instructional plan, to select the methods, strategies, questioning sequences, activities, materials and media, we must first select the specific process skill or sequence of process skills which our pupils will use and apply to the cognitive and affective content. Note the emphasis is on the *pupil use* of process skills. Our selection of the processes to be used will in turn determine the specific strategies, the questioning techniques, the kinds of pupil activities and how materials and media will be incorporated. *Process selection is a prerequisite to instructional planning.*

Given our sequential list of objectives and our list of eleven process skills ranging from simple association to concept formation, we assess each objective and identify what we consider to be the most effective process or processes to be used in conjunction with each objective.

Here an example is clearly in order. Let's use our sample unit. One of our objectives deals with the development of the concepts of forest and grassland. We could instruct for these concepts on a purely rote level minimizing the use of process. We could ask the pupil to "look-up" the terms and return with a written report on forest and grassland. The results are well-known to all of us. The pupil uses an encyclopedia or a comparable resource, "reads" and copies the specific page or pages and returns to feed back the unprocessed information. A Xerox machine would have been more efficient! Few of us today would take that instructional route. Many of us however would have the pupil utilize the text and assign the conventional questions to elicit the factual data. Again, for most pupils the results are the same, unprocessed information. However if we use the Behavioral Outcomes Approach focusing on the pupil as an active interactor and processer and we are not concerned with the instant acquisition of data whose retention is minimal, we will take another approach and a more gradual one. We may expose the pupils to photographs of forests and grasslands, have them view films and filmstrips, visit a forest and or grassland area, have them recount their own experiences in this context as well as what they have seen on TV or read in books. We would then focus on getting *them* to process this data by asking the pupils to *observe* each area, *compare* each of these areas, note the similarities and differences, *analyze* how these differences produce different effects and then *generalize* in terms of the effects on man's survival. In moving toward and into the affective domain, we would *sensitize* our pupils by having them interview people whose livelihoods depend on the growth and restoration of these areas, have them *analyze* the direct impact of the use and abuse of these areas on their daily lives and confront them with the issue on an action level, "What if anything can we *do*?"

The differences in approach cannot be ignored. In the first case, the pupil reads, copies and regurgitates. In the second case, the pupil, given an experiential base, observes, compares, analyzes, generalizes, is sensitized and is confronted with a real need for action. Here he is given ample opportunities *to process cognitively, affectively and to act.*

In sum, prior to any instructional planning, it is essential that we examine each objective and identify the various processes pupils will use in order to attain them. If—we ignore step 4 and work directly from the objective to the identification of methods, activities, strategies, materials and media, the number and kinds of processes we are likely to utilize will be limited. Teachers who have omitted the *process analysis* found that the instructional plans which emerged were not very different from what they had always been doing. They were quick to realize that the degree and diversity of process were the key variables. As one of these teachers expressed it, "Of course all good teachers have used process, but to what extent?"

Step 5—Specifying Methods, Strategies, Activities, Questioning Patterns, Materials and Media

Having completed process analysis, step 5, that of constructing an instructoinal plan presents no problems and flows naturally. Given the process and or sequence of processes for each objective, teachers reaily make the match between process and methodology. In constructing the learning units it is not necessary to rewrite the entire step-by-step questioning pattern of each of the process strateetegies. What is recorded is simply the name of the strategy by it General Interpretation, Affective Analysis or Critical Thinking Applied To The Affective Domain. Only in cases where teachers feel it is helpful are the initial key questions noted. To develop strategy competency, each of the strategies are placed on cards for classroom practice. Teachers become secure in their use and the resultant questioning patterns appear almost "intuitive."

The incorporation of materials and media is readily accomplished, for having identified the processes and the process strategies, the materials and media are then used *in that process context*. For example using our previous sample unit, if we are to develop concepts of forest and grassland via the processes of observation, comparison and analysis at the cognitive level, the films, filmstrips, photographs are used with the key structures of these strategies namely; what do you observe? What are the differences? Similarities? What relationships exist? etc. In the affective domain the adaptation is equally as smooth. Whether we are using a story or a set of incidents on film or a sound-filmstrip, the structures for the exploration of feelings, beliefs, analysis of values and behaviors are taken directly from the strategies.

To sum up, we have examined the following five basic steps used in constructing an affective-cognitive learning unit:

Step 1—Prepare a preface
Step 2—Constructing a content outline
Step 3—Specifying pupil objectives at the *four levels of* learning
Step 4—Selecting the process skills to be used in attaining the objectives
Step 5—Specifying methods, strategies, activities, questioning patterns, materials and media

To obtain a concrete picture of the total process and to fully understand how we synthesize the unit, let us look at the format as well as at sample pages of a unit. We have before us a preface page, a content outline of the entire unit and a list of specific pupil objectives. In addition for each objective, we have identified the process skill or skills which the pupils will use to attain the objective. The process strategies are available to us; we have only to refer to the listing on pages 40-43. For a more detailed description of each of the strategies, we may turn to Chapters 3, 4 and 5. The format we use is shown on page 172. The column headings designate what is to be placed in each column. The illustrations from a sample unit which follow the format sheet demonstrate how the teacher plans for the cognitive, affective and action levels in dealing with one concept. It goes without saying but—it is invaluable at the early stages of curricular modification to plan in detail. "Good" planning, detailed sufficiently to meet your own needs, insures successful implementation. Think back to your early years as a teacher, you planned to the nth degree. But as the years moved on, the details were internalized and your plans were written in general terms. In constructing affective-cognitive learning units, the same holds true. As teachers become more proficient and secure in operating at all four levels, details are minimized and only key strategies and activities are recorded. Being overly specific initially does serve as an excellent security blanket. But once you discard the blanket, the details are also discarded.

In the implementation process, teachers find themselves continuously modifying the plan and adapting it to the needs of specific groups of pupils. This is as it should be. We are matching these affective and cognitive units to our pupils affective and cognitive structures. It is essential that we view and utilize these plans in an *open* and *flexible* manner. If we utilize the plan realistically, *we will find that no two groups of pupils will operate in the same manner;* the variations of individual differences will be obvious.

Questions most frequently raised by teachers center on the length of the unit and the diversity of activities and resources. The length of the unit is essentially a function of the specific groups of pupils with which you are dealing. Attention span, pupil interests, ability to work in groups are all determining factors. As for the diversity of activities and resources, the greater the diversity, the more effective the unit. Since most of these units have been used in a

BEHAVIORAL OUTCOMES LEARNING UNIT
Integrating Affective and Cognitive Components

Unit Title _____:

Subject of Unit _____:

Grade Level(s) _____:

(Column 1) Content Outline	(Column 2) Pupil Objectives	(Column 3) Process Skills	(Column 4) Strategies, Activities, Materials & Media

BEHAVIORAL OUTCOMES LEARNING UNIT
Integrating Affective and Cognitive Components

Unit Title: "Why Bother About Soil Conservation?"
Subject of Unit: Conservation of Natural Resources (one unit of a series)
Grade Level (s): Intermediate (Grades 4, 5 and 6)

(Column 1) *Content Outline*	(Column 2) *Pupil Objectives*	(Column 3) *Process Skills*	(Column 4) *Strategies, Activities, Materials & Media*
Concept of Erosion (Cognitive Level)	Pupil will demonstrate his acquisition of the concept of erosion by: a. defining the process b. identifying the various means by which erosion takes place c. classifying means as natural or man-made d. describing the effects of soil erosion on man's survival	Observation Comparison Classification Generalization (Inductive Reasoning)	Observe film on erosion Compare different means of erosion Construct models demonstrating soil erosion Classify means of erosion Construct a generalization indicating relationship between erosion and its effects on man's survival

Concept of Erosion (Affective Level)	Pupil will demonstrate his sensitivity to and concern with the process of erosion and its effects on the community	Observation
		
		 Analysis
		
		 Affective Comparison
		
		 Affective Analysis
			Identify areas on the school grounds and in the community where erosion is evident. Interview people living in these areas or adjacent to them to discover how the situation affects them, what action they have taken, what obstacles confront them. Photograph these areas.
			 Discuss findings with classmates:
			    What attitudes do people have in relation to this problem?
			    What values are involved?
			    What conflicts of interests exist?
			    How can we bring about a change in attitudes, in values?

		Critical Thinking	What alternative course of action can we take? What are the pros and cons of each plan of action?
Concept of Erosion (Action Level)	Pupil will demonstrate valuing soil conservation by taking some constructive action in combating erosion	Analysis Critical Thinking . Analysis	Review areas on the school grounds and in the community where erosion is evident and select those where realistic action can be taken by the pupils. Identify agents of erosion and methods to remedy the situation.
		Critical Thinking	Consult with the city's Conservation Commission and community members to arrive at a plan of action in which pupils can realistically assist. Photograph the areas before implementing plan. Implement plan.
		Critical Thinking	Assess progress. Report on progress using diverse media (a) Letter to local newspapers (b) Release to local radio station (c) Display photographs (before and after) in local banks and shopping areas. (d) Visit other schools in the city and publicize what has been done

heterogeneous setting, teachers have included a large number of activities and a variety of media. However the *greatest thrust on diversity has been in the use of as many process skills as possible.* Research clearly indicates that *all pupils regardless of "IQ" scores and achievement scores are capable of using the process skills.* If we maximize the use of process skills, we maximize the opportunities for learning. How we achieve this is dealt with in the next section of this chapter.

At this point, it is important to point out that two additional components are part of the learning unit; namely the pre-test, to determine where the pupil is at the beginning of the unit and the post-test to determine whether the pupils have achieved the unit's objectives and to what extent. In this age of growing accountability, there is no need to point out the significance and practical utility of these tests. In reality, at the classroom level, we are moving toward a more systematic individualized process of instruction. In Chapter 9, we ai focus on a model which serves to accomplish just that. However, at this point, let us examine how teachers develop a "process" methodology, how they obtain a process profile of their teaching style and what changes if any they are able to effect.

Obtaining A Cognitive and Affective Process Profile of Your Teaching Style

No doubt volumes can be written on teaching style. In fact the number of research studies on teaching style have been overwhelming. The reason is obvious. Other than the pupil, the teacher is the key variable in the instructional setting. His or her knowledge, background, culture, personality, value system, expectations all contribute to that key variable, teaching style. We could readily resort to the "cop-out" of teaching as an art, as God's gift to education—and merely state that some possess this attribute or talent and others do not and so be it! Or we could view teaching as a science, a set of skills and behaviors which can be developed and improved. None of us will dispute the fact that there are individuals who appear to be "born" teachers. How many times have we seen a new addition to our staff and concluded, without the aid of the OSCAR I or OSCAR II or Flander's scale of Interaction Analysis or any other observation scale or matrix, that this person was "a natural." Intuitively we sensed it and so did the pupils.

Speaking only from an experiential base, as an experienced teacher and as a supervisor, these "naturals" or "born" teachers appear to have two outstanding traits which enable them to adopt and utilize "process" methodology readily. They display an openness and flexibility to changing conditions and an authentic receptivity to people. The key question which arises from this observation is simply, if—teachers who are open, flexible to change and receptive to individuals are readily able to utilize "process" methodology, is it possible that teachers who begin to and continue to use "process" methodology will modify their own behavior and become more open, more flexible to change and more receptive to pupils? Is this possible? Has it happened and to what extent? My response may be viewed as cautious, but it is realistic. These traits can be developed in most teachers to a significant extent. All? By no means! We are all aware of what I have called the unchanging "Rocks of Gibraltar" in teaching who resist change and will remain so despite our efforts—until drastic changes are made in our profession.

But let us return to the ability of teachers to modify their teaching styles, to use process methodology, to expand process methodology and in turn demonstrate behavioral changes. During a period of five years when the initial Behavioral Outcomes Approach was gaining momentum in the Norwalk Public Schools, behavioral change on the part of the staff was so clearly evident that supervisors and principals had no difficulty in identifying those teachers who were involved in the program. The so-called B.O. teacher was and is characterized by specific behaviors: listens to pupils, asks open-structured process-centered questions, limits teacher-talk, encourages pupil-talk, expands and clarifies pupil's ideas. Shades of Flander's high I/D teacher!

Teachers in the original program in Norwalk and the staffs of those school systems who used the modified approach incorporating the affective domain were strongly aware of the changes they were making in their behavior. Comments such as the following were frequently made: "I'm learning to talk less and listen more." "I've finally learned to pause, not to expect instant responses to process questions. I give the pupils time to get in touch with their feelings and thoughts." "The use of process in the affective domain has given me greater insights into my kids." "What I found most valuable was that liking kids was not as important as really understanding them!"

In sum, teachers can and do change their behaviors, their teaching style. However in order to do so, they had to have some method of diagnosing or identifying their own style. What they needed was a realistic profile of their teaching style. In some school systems where video taping equipment was available, teachers micro-taught, video taping ten minute segments of lessons using a small group of pupils and then analyzed their behavior.

In all schools using the modified Behavioral Outcomes Approach, teachers used a table of specifications. After constructing an affective-cognitive learning unit and prior to its classroom implementation, teachers analyzed their units in terms of the specific process skills and strategies they planned to use in the instructional process. The key question they asked was, "How many *different process strategies* have I incorporated in this unit in the affective and cognitive domains?"

On the whole, teachers found that they favored one or two processes in the past. Some found that they were inductive teachers always leading the flock to generalize. Others found that they constantly used analysis in the affective domain to the exclusion of all other processes. What became evident was the many teachers used process—but limited process.

The table of specifications is a grid consisting of a list of the process skills across the horizontal dimension of the chart and a list of the unit's objectives along the vertical dimension. The teacher, in analyzing the learning unit focuses on column 3, the process skills and in terms of each objective and process skill makes a tally using a letter C or an A on the grid. The C indicates that the particular process skill is being applied to the cognitive domain, the A indicates process application to the affective domain. As shown on page 178 the table of specification yields a total process profile. The teacher can readily see the number or range of processes being used in the unit and the extent to which they are being applied in each domain. The range or pattern is viewed as narrow if one to three processes are used in each domain. The broad pattern contains four or more processes in each domain.

On finding a narrow range, the teacher reviews the learning unit and modifies it by incorporating additional process skills or substituting over-used processes with others. The resultant learning unit is a multi-process affective and cognitive series of experiences promoting behavioral changes in both pupils and teachers.

It is as old as the hills, but as real as the hills: we learn from teaching. The most significant teaching skills you and I have acquired were not from Education 321.5 or 450.1 but from the actual classroom interactions. Whether we are Skinnerians or not, the behaviors we utilized in our classrooms were reinforced by success or extinguished by dismal failure. In implementing an affective-cognitive curriculum using process behaviors, expanding the use of these process behaviors by monitoring our process profile, we find that we are reinforced positively and that our teaching style does change. Teaching becomes a *processing process* and the over-all result is something many of us may have forgotten or discarded as a fantasy or an impossible dream. Teaching becomes that opportunity for greatness that Bel Kaufman speaks about; it becomes a stimulating exciting adventure filled with unpredictable positives and satisfactions derived only when adults and youngsters interact at the most relevant level—the process level.

To Summarize

In this chapter we have:

- re-substantiated the need for an affective-cognitive curriculum to bridge the gap between school and society and to confront the identity-values crisis
- detailed and illustrated "How to Construct Affective and Cognitive Learning Units"
- focused on the key to successful implementation—"process" methodology
- identified the role of the successful teacher as a processor of affective and cognitive knowledge
- provided a Table of Specification by which teachers may obtain a process profile of their teaching styles and modify their styles.

In essence, we now have the step-by-step procedures for curriculum development and a clear-cut understanding of our role in its implementation. In Chapter 9, we will deal with the fifth component of our blueprint that of "individualizing" an affective and cognitive curriculum.

To Obtain a Process Profile A Table of Specifications

PUPIL OBJECTIVES \ PROCESS	Observing	Associating	Comparing	Classifying	Analyzing	Interpreting	Generalizing	Divergent Thinking	Critical Thinking	Creative Thinking	Concept Formation
Given a variety of songs & poems: "This Land Is My Land" "Now That The Buffalo's Gone," the pupil will read & describe the message of each.					C						
The pupil will describe his feelings in terms of each song & poem		A			A						
The pupil will describe the feelings of the songwriter & poet					C						
The pupil will compare his feelings with those of the songwriter & poet			A								

The pupil will analyze the songs & poems, & identify the values of the songwriter & poet					A						
The pupil will compare his own values with those of the songwriter & poet			A								
The pupil will classify the songs & poems using values as criteria				A							

Broad Pattern   contains four or more processes
Narrow Pattern   contains one to three processes

9 Individualizing An Integrated Affective and Cognitive Curriculum With the Behavioral Outcomes Approach

Equipped with the sequential steps and format to modify our present curriculum and create affective and cognitive learning units, we are now prepared to implement this curriculum. In our implementation, we focus on another key component of our new blueprint for education—that of providing an instructional system that realistically individualizes at both the cognitive and affective levels of learning.

Like so many grandiose ideas in education, individualized instruction has received its share of misuses and abuse. In fact, more than its share, for it is the *innovation* of our decade. The advertising brochures, the articles in our professional magazines, the best sellers in education present us with the modern panacea—individualization. If—mind you—if we could individualize instruction, meet the needs of the individual child or to paraphrase Thoreau enable each child to step to the music of his own drummer, our problems would be solved—so we are told.

Individualization—A "Not-So-New" Concept

Again like so many "innovative" ideas in education, individualized instruction as a concept, and to some degree as a practice, is by no means new. We have only to recall the one-room schoolhouse of days gone by. Of course in those days, life was simple. One did not speak of a systems approach to education nor of an instructional management system. But—somehow that old-fashioned teacher in her one room schoolhouse, filled with children of different ages and varying abilities, did seem to "manage." If we were to attempt to describe her grouping practices and instructional methodology, using the educational jargon of today, we would probably say that to some degree—limited of course, she was operating within a hetergeneous setting and was attempting to implement a non-graded, self-paced, continuous progress program. Since she had no knowledge of homogeneous grouping, she was not likely to be frustrated with its absence. Although Individually Guided Education had not yet been conceived, she did attempt to guide and direct each child in terms of his individual differences in her small school. As for the problem of class size, she probably experienced it, if it were the case, but what recourse did she have? As for accountability, as all good teachers, she probably was very concerned about her pupils progress and felt accountable, did her best and did not experience future shock as to "who was going to hang who and who was going to do the hanging?"

But the point is—and it is quite obvious—that way back in those simple days—the concept of individualization was there—embryonic—but there—and that the teachers then, as in the present, were doing it to some extent!

My purpose in making this comparison requires some explanation. In every workshop which I have conducted on individualization, teachers make this point. Rightfully so and psychologically so, for it is natural for us to feel threatened by the new, the strange and the unfamiliar. But—once we assure ourselves that this is not the case—that it has always been there to some extent—we are able to move ahead more comfortably—the "newness" threat has been diminished.

None of us in our right minds, soft, hard or otherwise, question either the concept or the purposes of individualization. We are a nation of individuals. We have used the democratic process to insure this cherished and prized individuality. In this mechanistic and technological era, the need to maintain, sustain and foster our individuality, our self-identity, our sense of being unique appears far greater than ever before. The need to foster the development of our human resources so that individual abilities and potentials are realized at optimal levels is indeed crucial. The concept that we modify our schools so that they not only reflect this need, but that they promote it, is no longer questioned. As parents, as teachers and foremost as individuals, we are "all for it." But as practitioners, we ask the real question—Can it be done in our schools?

The Many Versions of Individualization

But before we ask the question "Can it be done in our own schools, within the context of existing conditions, favorable or unfavorable," we must ask and respond to a far more basic question. "What is it?" Practically speaking "What do we mean by individualization?" A simplistic question? No, for a funny thing happened to me on my way to individualization. I had completed extensive research on individualization under a foundation grant. As a result of this research, a new grant materialized which resulted in a regional "model" program to train teachers to individualize instruction in three different school systems. It was not too long before I made a startling discovery. As co-director of instruction and planning, I found myself with three diverse faculties, all of which were committed to individualization. A good beginning! But—as a total group—we had all fallen into the same trap. "Of course everyone of us knew what individualization was!" But when an initial survey was taken as to how one viewed this process and dialogues ensued, it became evident—glaringly evident, that there were almost as many versions of individualization as there were participants in the program. The diverse concepts of individualization ranged from the very simple to the idealistic pie-in-the-sky, utopian, never-to-be-attained models. This was our problem then and, as I work with school systems today, I find this is still the case.

Needed—An Operational Definition of Individualization

Before any of us can attempt to individualize any curriculum, affective or cognitive, we must start with an *operational* definition of the process of individualization. The common cliches of individualization are just that—common. We know children have individual differences—one day in the classroom substantiates this. We know that children should progress at their own pace—ideal, great! This reminds me of the conversation of two youngsters walking home from school and one says to the other, "I'm progressing at my own pace. At whose pace are you progressing at?" We know that children possess different learning styles and that some learn more effectively and efficiently via one modality rather than another. So what else is new? The point is that knowing all this does not enable the teacher or administrator to implement, or to "realize" individualization.

To "realize" individualization we start with the classroom. It is common knowledge that the key variables in any classroom are those pertaining to the teacher and the pupil. The key agent of instruction, the *individualizer* is the teacher. Logically we focus on the teacher and ask the key questions: "What does an individualizing teacher do?" "What does an individualizing teacher do that the conventional teacher does not?" and "What specific skills should an individualizing teacher possess?" Still further—"If you and I walked into an 'individualized' classroom, what would we expect to see—namely how would the teacher be functioning and what would the pupils be doing?"

To answer these questions, we devised an operational model focusing on the teacher and the pupil and specifying what constitutes individualizing teacher skills, how do pupils function in an individualizing setting and what specific entry behaviors or skills should pupils have to insure initial success in an individualizing setting.

In terms of the teacher's functions, we identified the key components of individualization. In a nut shell these components include:

Specific Pupil Objectives

Diagnosis

Teaching Strategies

Curricular Materials

Media

Grouping Practices

Record-Keeping Techniques

Reporting Devices.

In working with these components, the teacher functions at two levels, as a planner and as a doer. Let us review each component, the rationale for its inclusion and the "practicability" of each in terms of the problems which do arise.

Individualizing Teacher Skills

The individualizing teacher demonstrates skills in:

1. *The specification of pupil objectives in behavioral and/or performance and measurable terms.*
    Rationale: If education is to become individualized, we require a systematic and more precise description of what the pupils will be able to do as a result of instruction.
    Practical Aspects: No real problems exist. Teachers, as well as commercial producers of curricula, have and are specifying pupil

objectives. Objectives in the tool skills, cognitive and affective areas are available and implementable.

2. *The use of diagnostic and evaluative techniques and tests to assess the pupil's entry behavior and mastery of the objectives.*

    Rationale: If we are to meet the pupil's individual needs, we must first diagnose to identify those needs. Teaching in the dark or to-whom-it-may-concern has proven ineffective. Following instruction as has always been the case, it is essential that we test to determine the degree of pupil mastery. In addition, in numerous individualization programs, pupils are provided with self-tests, enabling them to assess their own progress and determine their readiness for the post-test.

    Practical Aspects: Again, no major problems exist. Teachers and commercial producers of curricula are producing pre-test items to identify whether pupils have the pre-requisite or entry behaviors to insure some degree of mastery of the objectives or if they have already mastered a specific objective. Few teachers, if any, question the value of pre-testing for it enables them to "target" teach. Experienced teachers have found that extensive pre-tests are unnecessary and that a few pre-test items will yield the data they need. In addition, many teachers have used the item analysis of standardized achievement tests to provide an over-all and yet useful profile of pupil needs.

    In terms of the pupil self-test and the post-test, no problems exist. Teacher-made post-tests are readily constructed. Teachers utilize their objectives and simply construct items which match these objectives. Two versions are made, one serving as the pupil self-test and the other as the post-test. In addition, most of the commercial programs on the market today include self-tests and post-tests.

3. *The use of a variety of teaching strategies to provide for differential instruction.*

    Rationale: Our experience clearly demonstrates that no one strategy is equally effective for all pupils. It is common knowledge that differential instruction requires the use of different strategies and techniques with different pupil groups.

    Practical Aspects: What is common knowledge is not common practice. Teachers have had great difficulty in matching the type of instruction to the specific pupils or groups of pupils. Research substantiates that although teachers may group on the basis of "ability," they still instruct all of these "different" groups *in the same way.* They may "water down" the curriculum for the "slow" groups and "enrich" it for the "gifted" groups but—*the strategies used are the same.* As teachers we know that grouping practices have a *significant impact* on differential instruction. This will be dealt with in item 6, the use of flexible grouping practices. However—the hard fact remains, different instructional strokes are essential for different folks.

4. *The use of a variety of curricular materials.*
   Rationale: We fully recognize the need for diverse materials for diverse pupils. The various kinds of difficulties and the wide range of differences need no documentation. Moreover, the crucial component of diagnosis requires a variety of curricular materials. Our diagnoses become "so what diagnoses" unless we have a variety of curricular prescriptions to fill these diagnosed needs.
   Practical Aspects: We cannot ignore the facts. To acquire, organize and use a variety of curricular materials requires funds to purchase these materials, time and effort on the part of the staff to select, modify and organize existing curricular resources so that they can be used for this purpose. My own experience has demonstrated that dedicated and committed teachers will undertake the initial tasks. However to support and sustain this implementation, funds are crucial.

5. *The varied use of diverse media.*
   Rationale: If we are to make the match between learning modality and instructional resources, a variety of combinations of media as well as different and creative uses of common media are essential.
   Practical Aspects: New and creative media approaches have been developed. We have no need to belabor this point. There is an increasing involvement on the part of teachers in producing media ranging from overhead transparencies, filmstrips to slide-tape presentations and video tapes. Pupil involvement in this area has grown tremendously. However, funds are essential to promote these types of involvement as well as to obtain some of relevent and creative products from the commercial sector.

6. *The use of flexible grouping practices based on pupil diagnosis.*
   Rationale: Grouping is a key factor contributing to the success of individualization. Given our objectives, we diagnose for a specific purpose. Can the pupil or can't he? Does the pupil or doesn't he? The results of the diagnosis determine which pupils are deficient in specific skills. Based on diagnosed results we determine the kinds and number of *temporary* pupil groups requiring specific instruction for the mastery of specific objectives. Once the pupil in a group attains this mastery, he moves out of the group into another group.
   Practical Aspects: In theory, flexible, temporary, functional grouping sounds great. In practice, to be blunt, teachers get uptight. In practice, it can be done—if we discard the myth of the

homogeneous class. The controversy of homogeneous vs. heterogeneous grouping has persisted much too long. We know that the homogeneous class is a myth. Pupils may be homogeneous in terms of specific needs, in terms of specific masteries. We have been and are operating on this premise. At the elementary level, teachers group pupils for reading and for mathematics. Nor is it unusual at this level for regrouping to take place when a few children have demonstrated significant progress. As we are well-aware, flexible grouping does not mean changing the groups twice a year, children are *continuously regrouped* as they progress. At the secondary level, generally speaking, in the past, teachers have been assigned to "homogeneous" groups based on the data obtained from "IQ" tests and achievement tests. The instructional trend in these situations, has been to use the shot-gun approach and teach the total group.

In recent years, recognizing the psychological damage resulting from these practices, numerous school systems have instituted heterogeneous grouping at the middle and junior high schools. Those of us who have spent many years at the secondary level with "homogeneous" "slow," "low," "average," "accelerated" groups have seen the effects of peer pressure and reinforcement. A vicious cycle had evolved. Successes reinforced successes and failures reinforced failures. But now, teachers are confronted with heterogeneous groups, with pupils demonstrating a wide range of skills. The shot-gun approach is blatantly inadequate. The curriculum has to be diversified for it serves few. Teachers are frustrated. They are required to operate in a *heterogeneous setting* and to divide pupils into *functional homogeneous groups* and instruct each of these groups within a given period of time. The problem is magnified when the range of heterogeneity is so great that the *number* of functional groups overwhelms the teacher. The problem however can be solved; *if*— and these *ifs* are the critical realities. If teachers have a reasonable number of functional groups, if teachers have diversified curricular strategies, materials and media, if pupils are prepared and taught to follow specific directions, to become more self-directive, to work in small groups. In sum, if a systematic carefully structured procedure for classroom management is used, teachers can function in this heterogeneous setting and also become effective individualizers. The key point which must be emphasized, to maintain a realistic perspective in terms of group instruction—and this will be expanded later on in this chapter—is that individualization does not rule out—by any means—*total class instruction or interaction.* Unfortunately individualization has become synonymous with a one to one instructional relationship and a small group process. The distortion can readily result in greater segregation and greater isolation and greater psychological damage than that which ensued from "ability" groupings. We seem to lose sight of the fact that homogeneous subgroups serve specific purposes in the *skill areas.* Individualization *in its most significant form* takes place *in a heterogeneous setting* in all other areas, enabling a *large group* of *pupils* to interact with relevant knowlege, concepts, issues and values. It enables diverse pupils to share and exchange ideas, feelings, values, to gain insights, to learn from each other, to serve as models for each other, and to develop healthy inter-personal relationships. To lose sight of this dimension of individualization is to reduce it to a mechanistic, depersonalized, sterile training program.

7. *The use of record-keeping techniques.*
   Rationale: If pupils are to master specific objectives based on diagnosed needs, progress at their own pace, in terms of their own learning styles, this should be recorded. What is required is a simple checklist so that a continuous pupil profile is constructed, identifying the objectives which have been mastered as well as those to be mastered.
   Practical Aspects: No problem exists in this area. Experience in individualization has indicated that these checklists should focus on the *major* objectives, require rapid check marks and brief notations. Numerous record-keeping devices have been constructed by school systems as well as by commercial producers and are readily adaptable.

8. *The use of reporting devices which clearly communicate pupil progress to parents and pupils.*
   Rationale: The framework of an individualized instructional system based on pupil objectives dictates a reporting device which focuses on these objectives.
   Practical Aspects: Therefore, an increasing number of school systems involved in individualization, have revised the old-fashioned report card and have replaced it with a listing of the major objectives of the disciplines as well as a brief description of the pupils's work habits and social-emotional development. However, this is not to say that grades have been eliminated. Although parents and pupils find this type of information meaningful, they still request the grades. Up to this point in time, the trend had been to attempt to move away from the "Wad-ja-get?" system of grading. However a reversal is already evident. Grades are being restored. In addition to the written report, conferencing is increasing and parents and teachers are obtaining a more realistic picture and appreciation of each others role.

To sum up at this point, one major dimension of our model focuses on the eight individualizing skills of the teacher, namely: specifying pupil objectives, diagnosing and evaluating, differentiating instruction by using a variety of teaching strategies and a variety of curricular materials and media, grouping and regrouping pupils based on specific needs in the skills area, and recording and reporting pupil progress. The teacher utilizes these skills in two stages; stage one in her role as a planner, and stage two in her role as an implementer, as shown on the chart on page 189. Before we apply this dimension of the model to the individualization of an affective and cognitive curriculum, let us turn to the other dimension of the model, the pupil, in terms of the skills he must have in order to function in and profit from an individualized environment.

The key variable is the pupil's ability to be self-directive. By self-directive we mean the pupil's ability to direct his learning and to evaluate his progress, namely, we are dealing with two components, self-instruction and self-evaluation.

The Essential Pupil Skills for Individualization—
Self-Instruction and Self-Evaluation

In making the transition from a traditional setting to one of individualization, we are compelled to face the realities—realities which many of us ideologically do not accept—but up to this point in time have been unable to alter. As our own experiences as pupils have clearly demonstrated and as is still the case today, conventional schools are characterized by a high degree of structure. In a highly structured environment, pupils are carefully taught—carefully taught to be more dependent than independent. Specific mind sets have been established. Conformity is prized. Independent thinkers and doers are rarely conformers. Pupils rapidly learn that conformity "pays off" in school. And so those who plan to succeed tend to become more dependent. Independence is submerged. Pupils become "adjusted" to being directed rather than directing their learning. They become accustomed to being led step-by-step. They not only expect, but they demand structure. As many of us have found, they are frustrated, fearful and lost when left on their own. Their learning—they believe—is a function of the teacher. That "old-fashioned" concept of learning-to-learn, which we view as critical, dies an early death. Self-direction has become teacher-direction. Self-instruction has become teacher-instruction and the process of education has become a school-directed process, rather than a person-directed process.

CHART I

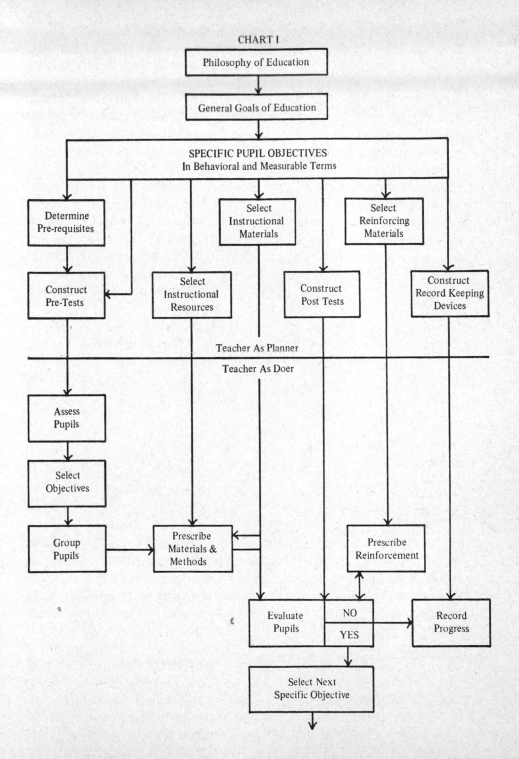

The second component of self-direction, equally vital to individualization is self-evaluation, namely the pupil's ability to assess both his cognitive and affective growth. For most pupils this requires a new set of behaviors in the classroom. Teachers have always marked their papers, identified errors, monitored their progress and behavior, and graded them. To ask pupils to monitor and assess their own progress is to change the rules of the game. To suddenly place them in a setting where the responsibility for learning *as they view it,* is shifted from the teacher to themselves can be and is frightening. As was pointed out in earlier chapters, telling the pupil he is free to think for himself, free to be himself and become himself, free to evaluate and take stock of himself, by no means enables him to do so. He has tried to become a model of a very model pupil and now we are asking him to become himself! Instruction and evaluation have been exclusively the roles of the teacher and now we are asking him to share in these roles. But unless the pupil shares in these roles, individualization will not take place.

The foregoing description may seem harsh but so is the reality. If we are to succeed in individualization, we must reverse this process, create a climate that is conducive to self-direction. We must provide opportunities to "let it happen," we must not be fearful of the "chaos" which we anticipate. The "chaos" is not the result of self-direction but the result of a lack of it. If we are striving for true individualization, not the ersatz variety depicted in popular articles and characterized by high structure, programmed steps and mechanistic and impersonalized instruction, then we must set the stage and provide the personal resources for self-direction "to happen."

The Seven Major Areas of Self-Direction

In describing the teacher dimension of our model, I have enumerated the specific teacher skills in terms of behaviors which he or she would demonstrate. In describing the pupil, the same procedure is followed. In an individualizing setting, the pupil demonstrates his ability to be self-directive in seven major areas, namely:

- Accepting and Performing Learning Tasks
- Following Directions
- Processing Cognitive and Affective Data
- Demonstrating Competency In and Responsibility For The Use of Curricular Materials and Equipment

- Working Toward Mastery
- Demonstrating Personal Effectiveness
- Demonstrating Social Effectiveness

Specific Self-Directive Pupil Behaviors

Let us examine each of these areas in terms of the specific pupil behaviors they subsume.

Accepting and Performing Learning Tasks

1. Accepts a specific objective as congruent with his needs.
2. Selects a learning task from a given number of alternatives offered by the teacher.
3. Plans how he will conduct the task.
4. Schedules his time for task completion.
5. Evaluates his progress as he works on the task.
6. Identifies problems he encounters and attempts to solve them with little or no assistance.
7. Seeks assistance when he is certain that he is unable to cope.
8. Alters his approach when necessary.
9. Persists in the task until completion.
10. Evaluates his achievement.
11. Discusses his performance with the teacher.

Following Directions

1. Demonstrates understanding of oral and written directions.
2. Applies these directions in performing tasks.
3. Evaluates his performance in terms of directions.

Processing Cognitive and Affective Data

1. Applies the process skills in developing concepts, in arriving at and testing generalizations and in synthesizing cognitive data.
2. Solves problems by exploring a *variety* of solutions rather than searching for one solution.
3. Questions rather than readily accepting answers at face value.

4. Readily admits to finding no solution when evidence is insufficient.

5. Takes risks in proposing novel or way-out ideas.

6. Applies process skills to affective data.

7. Freely accepts his own feelings and values as well as those of others.

8. Assists others in clarifying their feelings and values.

9. Takes a firm stand when his values are challenged.

Demonstrating Competency In And Responsibility For The Use of Curricular Materials and Equipment

1. Demonstrates knowledge of the proper use of materials.

2. Demonstrates skill in using equipment.

3. Repairs equipment.

4. Assumes responsibility in caring for materials and equipment.

Working Toward Mastery

1. Understands the rationale for performing tasks.

2. Understands the criteria for mastery.

3. Works toward mastery.

4. Assesses his progress utilizing the given criteria.

Demonstrating Personal Effectiveness

1. Demonstrates a sense of self-worth by establishing his own standards of performance.

2. Demonstrates pride in his accomplishments and in his appearance.

3. Expresses his views and opinions with confidence.

4. Makes personal decisions and assumes the responsibility for the consequence.

Demonstrating Social Effectiveness

1. Is sensitive to the feelings and opinions of others.

2. Readily offers assistance to others.

3. Works cooperatively with others to achieve a common goal.

4. Engages in group discussions and group decision-making.

5. Demonstrates respect for the person and belongings of others.

In sum, ideally for a pupil to function in an individualized setting, the foregoing self-directive behaviors are needed. At a practical level, as we gradually implement individualization, we provide opportunities for these behaviors to occur and for their reinforcement.

Applying The "III" Model to a Classroom Situation

Up to this point, a two-dimensional model has been presented— but models serve a purpose only if they are applied to a real situation. Recognizing the limits of a written description, let us transpose this model into an actual classroom. We are returning to some of our key questions—What would we expect to observe if we visited an individualizing classroom? What would the teacher be doing? How would the pupils function?

Since our focus is on the individualization of an integrated affective and cognitive curriculum, we will apply this model to a sample learning unit. The pupils will be operating at the four levels of learning described in Chapter 8, namely, the skills, knowledge, values and action levels. We will utilize the unit outlined in Chapter 8, "Why Bother About Soil Conservation?"

In this unit, you will recall, at the skills level we provide opportunities for the use of the 3R's, research skills and model building. At the knowledge or cognitive level, we seek to develop, via the process skills, the key concepts of soil, forest, grassland, erosion, drought and conservation as well as four generalizations dealing with man's dependency on the soil, the effects of natural phenomena on the loss of topsoil, man's use and abuse of these resources and man's efforts at protection and restoration. In the process of developing both concepts and generalizations, we plan to incorporate factual data.

Given a heterogeneous class of pupils, we start by administering a pre-test which may consist of 5 or 6 reactions. Each action deals with a specific area. For example, the first section may deal with the key concepts, the second with generalizations, the third with factual data, the fourth with some research skills and the fifth with values and interest in the specific topic (in this case, conservation). In this unit, the following pre-test was used. Although superficially it may appear lengthy, it takes no more than the usual time to administer and is easily assessed. In fact, both teachers and pupils find it a stimulating and clarifying experience. They both are obtaining a preview or the "Coming Attractions" of the unit in terms of each one's role.

Unit: *"Why Bother About Soil Conservation?"*

Part I. *Key Concepts*

A. On Table 1, you will find five samples of different materials. Observe each sample and below write the *number* of the sample which is soil.
The soil sample is number _____.

B. List two key ingredients of top soil.

C. List three major uses of soil.

D. On Table 2, you will find a set of five numbered pictures.

1. Identify the picture of a forest.
It is number _____.
2. Identify the picture of a grassland.
It is number _____.
3. List two ways in which a forest differs from a grassland.

E. On Table 3, you will find a set of five numbered pictures.

1. Identify the picture of an area which has been eroded.
It is number _____.
2. Identify the picture of an area which has been hit by a drought.
It is number _____.

F. On Table 4, you will find a set of six pictures. Two of these pictures illustrate good conservation practices. List the numbers of these pictures below:

They are number _____ and number _____.

Part II. *Generalizations*

Read each of generalizations given below. Next to each one, record whether you agree or disagree with each generalization and give one reason for each answer.

A. We are totally dependent upon our soil and land for our survival.

B. Natural phenomena have caused a loss of large quantities of topsoil and natural vegetation.

C. Man's abuse and misuse of soil, forests and grasslands have resulted in great losses of land.

D. Man can protect and restore his natural resources.

Part III.   *Factual Data*

On Table 5, there are ten pictures. Match these pictures with the items listed below by placing the number of each picture next to the item it illustrates. You will have two pictures left.

_____   a. minerals

_____   b. humas

_____   c. loam

_____   d. terracing

_____   e. contour plowing

_____   f. furrows

_____   g. cover crops

_____   h. controlled grazing

Part IV.   *Research Skills*

You are asked to find some information on contour plowing in the school library. Describe briefly how you would use the library to obtain this information.

Part V.   *Values and Interest in Conservation*

A.   How do you react to the following recommendations? If you are worried about a recommendation, place a *W* in front of it; If you are not concerned, place an *O* in front of it, and if you approve use an *A*.

A citizens' group in town has made the following recommendations:

_____ A large wetlands area in Brookville is a perfect location for a jetport.

_____ Cranbury Park should be used for a new housing project.

_____ The city purchases a few mini-buses to reduce the number of cars on the roads.

_____ The Cherry Lane swamp area should be filled and replaced with a new shopping center.

_____ The cost of maintaining lawns in public areas in the center of town is too expensive. All of this ground should be covered with concrete or asphalt.

B.   Check any of the following statements below in each of the categories which best applies to you.

_____ A (1)   I am definitely very interested in conservation.

_____ A (2)   I have some interest in conservation.

_____ A (3)   I really don't care about conservation.

_____ B (1)   I would volunteer to participate in a conservation action program.

_____ B (2)   I might consider participating in a conservation action program.

_____ B (3)   I would not participate in a conservation action program.

_____ C (1)   I feel I know a great deal about conservation.

_____ C (2)   I feel I have some knowledge about conservation and I would like to know more.

_____ C (3)   I feel I know very little about conservation.

Given this framework which will serve as a guide, we begin the unit with the total class. We may show a film on how man uses and abuses the soil. Pupils are then asked to break up into 4 or 5 discussion groups. Each group leader is given a set of questions, i.e., What factual data did you obtain from the film? What *generalizations can you* make from this film? What *kinds of questions* did the film prompt? What additional information would you seek? What kinds of feelings did the film evoke? What values or lack of values did it illustrate? How does what you viewed relate to our community? How does it affect you, or does it? If it does, what realistic action can you take?

Following small group discussions, the total class reassembles. A large group discussion ensues on the knowledge level. At this point the teacher structures questions so that pupils *process*—compare, analyze, induce generalizations, use divergent thinking. *During all large group discussions, process questions are used.* A record is made of the pupils' cognitive questions and of the additional data sought. Pupils are asked to select specific questions they wish to "research." They are free to form groups of three or a pupil may wish to work independently. Groups (of three or one) are asked to construct a plan of action, determine what kinds of resources they will use, how much time they will allocate to their knowledge search, how they will evaluate their efforts and how they will communicate their findings to the class using any mode they wish. At this point pupils who lack research skills may be grouped and are provided with instruction.

As each group or individual completes the knowledge search, each proceeds to the values search. Based on the data, pupils compile a list of values—centered issues to be discussed and explored.

The total class is again reassembled and groups or individual pupils share their findings of the knowledge search. At this point, the teacher utilizes the process strategies stimulating the pupils to analyze the data, view it from various perspectives, question its validity, exercise care in interpreting it, and exercise care in making inferences, and in applying it to specific situations. Given the *processed knowledge* base, the total class identifies the value-centered issues, and discusses these issues relating them to the community and individual. Pupils select those issues which they view as top priorities, debates ensue. Pupils are then asked to work in small groups or as individuals and select an issue, take a stand on the issue, and determine a realistic plan of action to confront this issue in some concrete manner. The use of the community and its resources is encouraged. The plan, as in the case of the knowledge search, emanates from the group. The group identifies the issue, the resources, the time schedule, funds needed, outside agencies involved, the method of communication of the results as well as this method of evaluation.

As groups complete their action projects, they schedule their "presentations" for the total class. Class members are constantly asked to review action projects, provide suggestions for improvement and serve as consultants to other groups.

Throughout this unit the teacher serves as a guide, a skills reinforcer, a resource person. A post-test is given to determine mastery of the knowledge components of the unit.

If we analyze the pupil behavior in this unit, we find that he interacts in a large group setting, a small group setting, as an individual if he so chooses. He selects a variety of materials and resources in-class as well as community resources. He is self-directive. He has the opportunity to interact freely with his *class community* at the cognitive, affective and action levels. He has the opportunity to reinforce his tool skills. The kind of individualized instruction which we view here should be designated not as I.I. but I.I.I., individualized inquiry-centered instruction. The inquiry component is not limited to the process skills being applied to the cognitive domain alone but to the affective domain as well.

The basic model of individualization is quite obvious when applied to affective and cognitive learning units. But what is equally obvious is that the application of the process skills in both domains and the extensive opportunities for pupil-pupil interaction makes this type of individualization a *living, ever-changing dynamic process* rather than a sterile mechanistic one for all concerned.

Summary

In essence, what has been detailed in this chapter has been a down-to-earth approach to individualization. We recognize that the concept of individualization is by no means original or new, that the need for a systematized but personalized approach to education is real, that an operational model describing teacher and pupil behaviors can be utilized provided resources are available, that the incorporation of the Behavioral Outcome Approach which focus on the pupil's use of process skills in the cognitive and affective domain within an individualizing framework serves to put the inquiry into individualization and prevents this process from deteriorating into a training approach. Individualizing affective and cognitive curricula with the Behavioral Outcomes Approach is a *total learning approach*.

10 Strategies for Starting

At this point in time, all aspects of the Modified Behavioral Outcomes Approach have been described in detail. We are now equipped with a new blueprint for education, an operational definition of self-concept, the process skills which are applicable to both the affective and cognitive domains, the step-by-step strategies for each of the process skills, highly specific guidelines in constructing behavioral objectives in the affective domain, realistic and positive means of assessing affective growth, clear-cut procedures for constructing affective and cognitive learning units and a practicalized procedure for individualizing instruction that focuses on both cognitive and affective learning and eliminates the mechanistic aspects inherent in present practices. We "understand" at both the cognitive and gut levels the rationale for this approach and, hopefully, we have developed a strong commitment to this program. Therefore, we are now at the most relevant point of the continuum—that of implementing the approach in our own schools with our pupils. We are viewing education as a process which seeks to promote the affective and cognitive growth of the individual. In this way, and only in this way, can we renew our schools so that they become "Schools for Children," rather than perpetuating what we have experienced, namely, "Children for Schools."

In order to initiate this approach and to experience a large measure of success at the early stages of implementation, the following strategies for starting are presented. These strategies are directed at both teachers and administrators, and should serve as guidelines to develop the approach gradually and systematically so that competencies in all aspects of the program result prior to total implementation.

Practical Guidelines for Teachers

Step 1. Select a Content Area and Brainstorm this Area Cognitively and Affectively

If you are an elementary teacher, select a content area in which you are most competent. If you are a secondary teacher, you are most likely a specialist in one or more areas. Specialist or generalist, be wise. Select a unit of study in which you are knowledgeable and about which you are enthusiastic. Brainstorm the content by identifying the key concepts, generalizations and relevant facts which the pupil should acquire in order to operate from a sound base of knowledge. Continue brainstorming, but this time from an affective perspective. What personal value does this content have for the youngster? Why am I teaching it and why should he learn these concepts? Why do I care about them and, more importantly, at his age level, in his surroundings, why should he care about them? How can I enable him to feel, to experience, to bring forth from his own previous experiences, the intrinsic values of these concepts? In what kind of "living" framework can we process these concepts so that feelings, beliefs, attitudes, and values are brought into the open? On the action level, what can these pupils do that will translate these values into real experiences? As a result of brainstorming, we are equipped with an outline of the key concepts, generalizations, facts, values and action-centered activities which will constitute this unit of study. In sum, we have pinpointed the cognitive and affective data the pupil will process.

Step 2. Develop Skill in Utilizing the Process Skills in the Cognitive Domain

Working with the content area you have outlined, begin to develop skill in using the structured questions for each of the process skills. Start by applying these process skills to the cognitige domain. The reason is obvious, for we want the pupils to operate from a base of knowledge. Concentrate you efforts by using two or three process skills per week. Focus on listening to your pupils' responses. Give them ample time to respond. If you are accustomed, as most of us were, to instant replies, screech to a halt. Use "pausing" behavior. Ask a question and pause. Explain to your pupils that the pause is to provide them with time to think about their responses so that they can express their own thoughts completely. If you feel uneasy and the process appears to be slow, don't be concerned. You are experiencing what we have all experienced. To use the vernacular, "Hang loose." Both you and your pupils are experiencing a new process, and it does take time, but the results are well worth it!

Keep in mind that you are using this unit as a pilot unit to practice process. Take the time to practice each of the processes. Many of them such as observing, associating, comparing and classifying, will be mastered readily. Processes, such as generalizing, analyzing and critical thinking, will take more time. Be prepared for exciting and stimulating interactions with your pupils.

Step 3.   Develop Competency in Utilizing the Process Skills in the Affective Domain

Having applied these processes in the cognitive domain, you will find that you are now structuring questions almost "intuitively." In developing competency with the process skills in the affective domain, use the same procedure as in Step 2. Focus on two or three processes per week. The most important factor at this point is to maintain an open, responsive classroom climate. Responses in the affective domain are neither right nor wrong nor good nor bad. They merely indicate how your pupils feel, view, value or do not value a specific situation. Make no attempt to change or have them change their responses, simply *accept* them. This same climate is essential to cognitive processing. Primary and intermediate pupils will initially respond well. They will be open in their responses. Secondary pupils will go through a period of adjustment. The name of the game has been the right answer, so they will have to be convinced that this is real and that no hidden agenda exists. Maintain a soft, low key atmostphere In less than a month, secondary pupils become well aware that the approach is authentic, and that cognitive and affective ping-pong is not being played. The idea that I, the pupil, must think as the teacher does, or feel or value as the teacher does, is rapidly dispelled. Listening on the part of the teacher is crucial at this stage. You will be continuously amazed at the kinds of information you are gathering about the individual pupils, and how you are "intuitively" using this information when you begin to individualize instruction. Affective processing will provide you with insights that have a direct impact on your instructional style with specific pupils. The effects on pupils are far more dramatic in terms of self-awareness and self-understanding.

Step 4.   Create and Maintain a Responsive Environment

Construct a checklist of factors which foster a responsive environment. Some of these factors (see Chapter 2) include an open climate, an atmosphere that is accepting, clarifying and promotes maximum pupil-pupil interaction. Concentrate your efforts on these factors. Tape and video-tape recorders have been our most useful mirrors in monitoring our own behavior. Many of us were amazed at the discrepancies which existed between what we assumed we were doing and how we appeared to our pupils, and how we actually were operating in the classroom. By using the checklist in conjunction with our tapes and reviewing our tapes privately, we were able to analyze our behavioral patterns and clearly identify changes as they took place. This procedure was threat-free, for we could view the tapes alone and then erase them. In many cases as we continued the process, we teamed with other members of the staff and reacted to each other's tapes. However, the choice was ours.

Step 5. Construct a Brief Affective and Cognitive Learning Unit

Having developed some proficiency with the process skills in both the affective and cognitive domains and fostered a responsive climate, construct a learning unit of one-to-two weeks' duration. Prepare a brief preface, outline the content at both the cognitive and affective levels, specify the pupil objectives, select the process skills you will use in attaining the objectives and identify the strategies and materials you will incorporate in the unit. *Using these few objectives as a framework,* construct a short pre-test and post-test. To check the range of processes you are using, construct a table of specifications and determine your process profile at this stage.

Step 6. Prepare Your Pupils for the Pre-test

The pre-test will not be a traumatic experience for your pupils if a clear-cut explanation of its purpose is provided. In fact, our experiences to date show that pupils enjoy the pre-test and become enthusiastic about the unit. Teachers have done an excellent job in explaining that the pre-test is merely a survey of pupils' knowledge, attitudes, interests and values and serves to enable the teacher to tailor the unit to their specific needs. This is readily accepted. In some instances, pupils and teachers have cooperated in assessing pre-test results and in identifying needs.

Step 7. Pre-test, Analyze Results and Modify Unit

Pre-test the pupils, analyze the results, tailor the unit based on your data and group you pupils in terms of their needs.

Step 8. Implement the Learning Unit

Utilize the learning unit; allow each group of pupils to work on their objectives. Make certain that all resources in the unit are readily available. Guide and assist in both large and small group instruction as needed.

Step 9.   Post-test

As each group of pupils completes the unit, administer the post-test items based on the unit's specific objectives. The post-test should reflect the various levels of the unit. For example, on the cognitive level, the post-test may require pupils to demonstrate their knowledge of a generalization by *applying it to a new situation;* on the tool skills level, the pupil may be required to read a short article on one of the issues dealt with in the unit and summarize the writer's point of view; on the values level, the pupil may select again one of the unit's issues and describe his stand on the issue and, finally, on the action level, the pupil might present an account of his activities and the relevance or lack of relevance his project had for him.

Step 10.   Provide Pupils with Knowledge of Results

A good testing situation is a good teaching situation. It is of dual value to review the results of the post-test with your pupils. Not only will the pupils know what they have and have not yet mastered, but they will have the opportunity to review the unit, clarify any misconceptions and determine, with the teacher's assistance, the areas which require further work. In addition, they are given the opportunity to provide inputs in evaluating their own progress, and this is crucial to further individualization.

Step 11.   Continue the Process of Unit Construction

As you observe the results of this approach with your pupils, you will develop a case of "Positive Addiction" to the process approach. You will find it extremely difficult to regress to old methods for the stimulation and the challenges encountered in affective-cognitive instruction and learning will promote a chain-reaction. This is the time to continue to modify curricular units and to develop expertise in process skills. The majority of teachers working with this approach found that after completing three or four units, they were well-prepared for the final step, utilizing the approach within a more formal individualizing framework.

Step 12.   Implement Affective-Cognitive Learning Units within an Individualizing Setting

At this stage, individualizing the learning units is a relatively easy and natural task. For in essence, we have already incorporated the key factors of individualization, namely, specific pupil objectives, diagnosis in the form of pretests and affective interactions which provided a wealth of significant data on pupils as individuals, process strategies promoting individual responses, curricular materials and media which may require greater diversification and grouping practices based on needs to attain specific objectives rather than nebulous scores. We have indeed come a long way. What we require now is to identify a great number of curricular materials and to devise simple record-keeping techniques and reporting devices. These tasks are again simple. Teachers prepare a sheet for each pupil, list the number or numbers of objectives and note the specific resources and activities used to attain these objectives. This constitutes the record-keeping device. In reporting pupil progress, a list of objectives is prepared and teachers and pupils cooperatively assess whether mastery has been attained.

The second aspect of individualizing at step 12 focuses on pupil behaviors. What has proved most useful has been the checklist of the sevan major areas of self-direction (see p. 190). Each pupil assists the teacher in assessing his ability to be self-directive in these areas and identifies those areas requiring reinforcement. The results have been extremely positive. Pupils accept these responsibilities and work hard at these tasks. Their relevancy does not escape them!

In sum, these twelve guidelines and, most importantly, the resources provided in this book should enable us to achieve our goal. The behavioral outcomes of this approach for teachers and for pupils will determine the future course of action. I have faith in both and, therefore, the future course of action is evident.

Practical Guidelines for Administrators

The guidelines and resources provided will enable teachers in all content areas and at all educational levels to utilize the Modified Behavioral Outcomes Approach and to fully implement an integrated affective and cognitive curriculum. However, we must not lose sight of the vital role of the administrator in the implementation process. When we speak of the administrator, we are not merely speaking of the program's director or the key consultant, we are identifying a group of individuals, namely, school principals, curriculum supervisors, central office staff including the assistant superintendents, the director of research, as well as the superintendent of schools. All of these individuals play a major role in the successful implementation and stabilization of a new program. In the majority of cases, only when the administrative and teaching staff work as a cohesive team does the new program survive the innovative stage and become incorporated into the school or school system at large.

In the Modified Behavioral Outcomes Approach developed in New York and expanded in a variety of New Jersey communities, as well as in the original Norwalk Plan, the successful outcomes of the approach could be attributed to two major factors, the commitment and involvement of the teaching staffs and extensive "support" of the administrative staffs. Focusing on the administrative behavioral patterns of those school systems which were successful in implementing the program, it is evident that commonalities exist. These are set forth as guidelines for the administrator. There is little doubt, based on my experience, that they are significant.

Guideline 1.   Demonstrate in-depth rather than superficial involvement in the program.

Principals, supervisors, assistant superintendents and, in a few cases, superintendents were active participants in the workshop sessions. They rolled up their sleeves and worked side-by-side with their teachers in experiencing process, in constructing behavioral objectives, in writing affective and cognitive learning units and in classroom testing these units. They "borrowed" classes and experienced the total process. As one principal remarked, "I certainly know how hard my teachers are working. We are in there together. They have seen me fall flat on my face, and I have seen them struggle." The kind and degree of cohesiveness which developed in these cases cannot be matched, for it emerged from both shared successes and shared failures. These administrators were sensitized to all of the operational aspects of the program. As a result of this, they were capable of giving concrete and realistic assistance which was valued by their staffs. When administrators spoke at PTA meetings or to community groups, the attitude of "What-does-he-or-she-know-about-this-program?" was non-existant. We knew he or she knew! There was no doubt about it!

Guideline 2.   All participants were accepted and respected as unique and competent individuals.

In all of the communities involved, the workshops on individualization, as well as those on the affective domain, clearly highlighted teacher diversity. Discussion and dialogue flowed. As a result of this open exchange, it was obvious that different individuals demonstrated competencies and expertise in different areas. This was acknowledged by group members and resulted in not only enhanced self-concepts, but in shared leadership and responsibility, which brings us to the next guideline.

Guideline 3.   Ample opportunities were provided for shared leadership and shared responsibility.

It was obvious as participants interacted and as problems arose that a variety of leaders emerged in different contexts. These individuals were freely given the leadership roles. What resulted may be viewed as a Hawthorne effect, for it became quite clear that all of us were responsible for the outcomes of this program. It no longer rested with the formal leadership alone. Teachers did not view themselves as cogs in the educational machine, but knew that they were valuable resources, People seemed to work harder, invest themselves in the program and derived obvious satisfaction.

Guideline 4.   Teachers were involved in the decision-making process.

In the majority of these communities, and this appeared to be prevalent in those who were attaining a high degree of success, administrators involved the teachers in the decision-making process. Teacher inputs were welcomed and utilized. As one teacher expressed it, "I don't feel directed or controlled. We level with each other and we've learned to tune in on each other. We know when we are acting in an "advisory" capacity and when our suggestions will be used. There is a balance here, and it is a healthy one."

Guideline 5.   Administrators demonstrated a high degree of responsiveness to the personal needs and problems of the staff.

Possibly this guideline incorporates aspects of guidelines 2, 3 and 4, but what appeared to be common to all of schools, where enthusiasm and satisfaction were high and progress was made, was the leadership style of the principals. In educational jargon we might say they were low-task, and high-relationship. But in concrete terms, they clearly communicated that they cared about their teachers, spent time discussing individuals' problems, allowed teachers to try out their own ideas and plans and were adept at minimizing conflicts. In brief, they clearly conveyed that people mattered first and foremost. In essence, it appears that behaviorally-oriented teachers supported by behaviorally-oriented administrators is the most desirable combination.

In a number of schools, teachers intrigued with the approach planted the seeds, and responsive and perceptive administrators nurtured their efforts. In other schools, the administrator initiated the approach and was supported by an open and flexible staff. What is of significance is not who initiated the approach, but that the approach was successfully implemented and the pupils reaped the rewards.

Concluding Statements

As I look back to my early days in education, when I went "up-the-down-staircase" in the forties and I assess the progress we have made to date, I am firmly convinced that we have the knowledge and tools to provide our children with and education that is of most worth—of most worth to the individual—of most worth to society—and one that will foster both role and goal development. We can create an identity society—one that identifies with the success of the whole individual. The skeptic will question, "Can we achieve this?" The realistic will reply, "Dare we fail?"

Bibliography

Ahmann, J. Stanley & M.D. Glock. *Evaluating Pupil Growth.* Boston: Allyn & Bacon, 1963.

Bloom, Benjamin S., J.T. Hastings & G.F. Madaus. *Handbook On Formative And Summative Evaluation Of Student Learning.* New York: McGraw-Hill, 1972.

Bloom, Benjamin S. et.al. *Taxonomy of Educational Objectives.* Handbook 1: Cognitive Domain. New York: David Mc Kay, 1956.

Gagne Robert M. *Learning and Individual Differences.* Columbus, Ohio: Charles E. Merrill, 1967.

Gagne, Robert M. *The Conditions of Learning.* New York: Holt, Rinehart & Winston, 1965.

Gerhard, Muriel. *Effective Teaching Strategies With The Behavioral Outcomes Approach.* West Nyack, New Jersey: Parker Publishing Company, Inc., 1971.

Glasser William. *Reality Therapy.* New York: Harper & Row, 1965.

Glasser, William. *Schools Without Failure.* New York: Harper & Row, 1969.

Glasser, William. *The Identity Society.* New York: Harper & Row, 1972.

Kibler, Robert et.al. *Behavioral Objectives And Instruction.* Boston; Allyn & Bacon, 1970

Kirschenbaum, Howard, Sidney Simon, *Wad-Ja-Get?* The Grading Game in American Education, New York: Hart Publishing, 1971.

Lindvall, C.M. *Defining Educational Objectives.* University of Pittsburgh Press, 1964.

Mager, Robert *Preparing Instructional Objectives*. Palo Alto, California: Fearon Publishers, 1962.

Popham, James et. al. *Systematic Instruction*. Englewood Cliffs, New Jersey: Prentice-Hall, 1970.

Postman, Neil & C. Weingartner. *Teaching As A Subversive Activity*. New York: Delacorte Press, 1969.

Postman, Neil & C. Weingartner. *The School Book*. New York: Delacorte Press, 1973.

Raths, Louis et.al. *Vaues And Teaching*. Columbus, Ohio: Charles E. Merrill, 1965.

Sanders, Norris *Classroom Questions—What Kinds?* New York: Harper & Row, 1966.

Silberman, Charles *Crisis In The Classroom*. New York: Random House, 1970.

Simon Sidney et.al *Values Clarification*. New York: Hart Publishing, 1972.

Taba, Hilda *Curriculum Development—Theory and Practice*. New York: Harcourt, World, 1962.

Weinstein, Gerald & M. Fantini. *Toward Humanistic Education—A Curriculum of Affect*. New York: Praeger Publisher, 1970.

Index

A

Ability, 184, 187
About Me, 154, 155
Accelerated groups, 186
Acceptance, 40
Accountability, 119
Achievement tests, 184, 186
Action, 48-49
Activators of behavior, 34
Activities, learning units, 170
Administrators:
    in-depth involvement, 205
    responsive to personal needs and
        problems of staff, 206-207
    shared leadership, 206
    shared responsibility, 206
    teachers involved in decision-making,
        206
    unique, competent participants,
        205-206
Affective behaviors, 21-23, 133
Affluence, 38
Alternatives, 35, 36
Analyzing:
    affective domain, 76-80
    breaking problem into component
        parts, 76
    cognitive domain, 76
    curricular content, 79-80
    definition, 46-47, 76
    general, 76
    identifying affective components, 77
    identifying relationships, 78
    identifying values hierarchies, 77
    relationships and interrelationships, 76
    selecting content, 78
    sequence or hierarchy of parts, 76
    strategies, 77-80
    structuring questions, 76-77
Anno, Mitsumasa, 85
Appearance, pride, 192
Application, 144
Arnold, Magda, 30
Assessment, instruments, 125, 153
Assistance:
    continuous, 160
    seeking, 191
Associating, definition, 46
Association:
    affective, strategies, 58-62

Association, *(cont.)*
    affective, structuring questions, 56
    controlled, 54
    curricular content, 60
    dual tool, 55
    effects, 55-56
    feelings, thoughts, behaviors, 59
    free, 53-54
    general, structuring questions, 56
    kinds, 53-55
    linked, 54-55
    operational definition, 53
    person content, 59-60
    promote self-concept, 56
'Attack and defend' strategy, 42
Attitudes, 27, 48, 154
"Attribute nonpossessor," 141
Authoritarian-centered method, 26
Autonomy:
    developing, 35-36
    dominative pupils, 37
    educating for, 36-38
    guide and tailor, 37
    identify with, term, 37
    integrative pupils, 37
    models for young, 37
    motivation and discipline, 36
    options and alternatives, 35, 36
    schools do little to foster, 35
    structure and support, 37
Average group, 186

B

Baker, Eva, 141
"Basics," 19
Beatty, Walcott, 30, 31
Behavior:
    affective, 21-23, 133
    classifying, 71
    cognitive, 21-23, 133
    comparing, 66
    definition, 48, 59, 129
    designating, 124, 128-130
    modification, 34
    overt and covert, 125, 130-132
    pausing, 200
    psychomotor, 133
Behavioral change, 24
Behavioral mix, unmixing, 125, 132-136
Behavioral objectives, 119